ORDNANCE SURVEY LEISURE GUIDE

SCOTTISH HIGHLANDS

▲ Kirkwynd Cottages, the Angus Folk Museum, Glamis

Produced jointly by the Publishing Division of
The Automobile Association and the Ordnance Survey

Editorial contributors: Stewart Angus (Walks); Hamish Brown (Walks); Alexander Cameron (Highlands History); Ross Finlay (Gazetteer); Barry Francis (The Games); Lynn ten Kate (Life on Skye); Peter MacAuley (Highlands by the Sea); Finlay J MacDonald (Spreading their Wings); Peter Marren (Wilderness Wildlife); Dr Robert J Price (Mountain Landscapes); Roger Smith (revisions to Features and Gazetteer, Tours and Walks); Rebecca Snelling (Fact File); Alex Sutherland (Walks).

Original photography: Dennis Hardley, Ronald W Weir and Jim Carnie

Typeset by Servis Filmsetting, Manchester
Colour separation by Mullis Morgan Ltd., London
Printed and bound by William Clowes Limited, Beccles and London

Maps extracted from the Ordnance Survey's 1:625 000 Routeplanner enlarged to 1:500 000, 1:25 000 Pathfinder Series, 1:250 000 Routemaster Series, and the Automobile Association's 1:1 000 000 Map of Great Britain reduced to 1:1 250 000. Reproduced with the permission of Her Majesty's Stationery Office. Crown copyright.

Additions to the maps by the Cartographic Department of The Automobile Association and the Ordnance Survey.

Produced by the Publishing Division of The Automobile Association.

Distributed in the United Kingdom by the Ordnance Survey, Southampton, and the Publishing Division of The Automobile Association, Fanum House, Basingstoke, Hampshire RG21 2EA.

First edition 1986
Reprinted 1987, 1989, 1990
Revised edition 1992

AA ISBN 0 7495 0387 4 (hardback)
AA ISBN 0 7495 0377 7 (softback)
OS ISBN 0 319 00286 1 (hardback)
OS ISBN 0 319 00277 2 (softback)

Published by The Automobile Association and the Ordnance Survey.

Introduction: Mallaig harbour

Caution

The walks in this book are over private land and do not necessarily follow public rights of way. While landowners usually do not mind visitors using defined routes, care must be taken to ensure that no damage or nuisance is caused to property or wildlife.

It is always advisable to go well-equipped with suitable clothing and refreshments when walking in the Scottish Highlands. The weather can change rapidly, and although most of the walks in this book are not arduous, no walk should be undertaken in adverse conditions.

Contents

▲ Glencoe

Introduction

Think of the Scottish Highlands and you instantly conjure up a vista of heather-clad hills, moody mountains and sparkling lochs, and catch the scented air of open spaces and lofty pines. The guide explores this treasure-house of nature and provides the key to appreciate the many breathtaking attractions in the region. The book traces the history, traditions and geology, lists and describes the towns, villages and hamlets, and offers a wide selection of walks and motor tours to seek out the finest scenery. Written entirely by people who know the region intimately, and backed by the AA's research expertise and the Ordnance Survey's mapping, this guide is as useful to the faithful who return to the Scottish Highlands over and over again as to the first-time visitor.

Highlands History

cottish mountains and glens may be magnificent to view but as places to make a living, they are a harsher environment, different and separate from the Lowlands. Highlands people were considered different, too, as long ago as 1521 when John Major, a Lowlander, called them 'Wild Scots' who spoke the Irish tongue (meaning Gaelic) and kept cattle and sheep. They were always keen for a fight, compared with the Lowlanders who spoke English and were quiet and more civilised, he thought, calling them 'householding Scots'. Yet he praised the Highlanders for their musical tradition using the harp, and particularly for their great love of singing.

People who came by sea

Early people found it much easier to enter the Highlands from the sea. The earliest, of some 5000 to 6000 years ago, have been traced to caves near Oban, where they survived by eating shellfish from the shore and by fishing.

Orkney, only a few miles north of the mainland, was particularly attractive to early settlers – we know that from the abundance of remains to be seen there today. Their houses at Skara Brae were lived in for over 600 years from 3100–2450BC, then covered in sand in a storm and miraculously preserved until they were revealed by another great storm in 1850. The stone houses have a bed on each side of a central hearth; even the furniture, such as the beds and dressers, survives because it was made of stone. Not far away is Maes Howe, the great chambered tomb the settlers built earlier than the Pyramids in Egypt, so big that it is possible to stand up inside and see the chambers in which the family of a great chief was buried. Near it they erected the Ring of Brodgar, a circle

Part of the ornate 7th-century Book of Kells (gospels)

of 60 massive stones, as their place for festivals, on midsummer's day, for example. Similarities in the diameter of this circle and circles at Avebury and the patterns on their pottery connect these farmer-fishers in Orkney with Avebury and Stonehenge in the south of England and they are as early in date.

The Great Glen, which offers a good way across the Highlands by Loch Lochy, Loch Oich and Loch Ness because it never rises much above 100ft, must have been used quite early. At Corriemony, up from Loch Ness, is a chambered cairn inside a circle of 11 standing stones, and at Clava, east of Inverness, are standing stones and chambered cairns, two with entrances aligned on the point where the sun sets on midwinter's day. Kilmartin, not far from the sea in mid-Argyll, also has a remarkable concentration of standing stones and burial cairns. The people who built them understood the calendar, the cardinal points of the compass and had the technology to move large stones close on 5000 years ago: not activities normally conjured up by the term 'wild Scots'.

Stone axes and gold ornaments originating in Ireland but found in the Highlands prove a trading connection lasting all through the bronze age (until about 500BC). Before this, climatic changes to colder and wetter weather restricted the amount of land that could be farmed and saw people fighting for the better land. In the east,

Remains of the enigmatic stone circle at Ben Langas

Blair Castle, founded by the powerful Comyn family

people built forts on hills and erected stone walls on a timber framework all round to protect themselves. Several of these were burned, but whether this happened accidentally or was done deliberately, and by whom, are still open questions. Whatever the reason, they burnt at such intense heat that the stones melted and joined together in a solid mass. Two of these vitrified forts worth visiting are Craig Phadrig near Inverness and Tap o' Noth, 1851 ft up near Rhynie in Grampian region.

About 100 BC an exciting new kind of stronghold began to appear in the west and north, close to the coast. This was the broch, a round stone tower with double hollow walls, which allowed it to rise to 40 ft or more. It has no weak point on the outside, and inside, where there was usually a well, people had a fire to cook on and room to sleep in, safe from the arrow or the hurled spear of the enemy outside. There are no brochs anywhere else in Europe but there are 500 in Scotland. The best examples to visit are Dun Telve and Dun Troddan close together in Glenelg, Dundorilla, close to the north coast, and Struanmore in Skye.

The broch-builders were probably Britons who came by sea from south Britain in the turbulent period before Julius Caesar came. When the Romans entered Scotland they came by land. In the north-east under Agricola they defeated the Caledonians, who must have been mainly Highlanders, in AD 84 at *Mons Graupius*, somewhere close to the Highland Line. The Romans wisely avoided entering the Highland passes and visitors will not see anything Roman in the Highlands. On the other hand, Highlanders occasionally attacked Roman Britain. A Roman writer called them *Picti*, 'the painted men', in

AD 297 and all the people in the Highlands came to be known as the Picts until new invaders arrived.

These were the Scots who crossed from Ireland in the 5th and 6th centuries AD and settled in Argyll which became Dalriada, the kingdom of the Scots. They chose *Dunadd*, a fort near Kilmartin, as their capital. On top is a footprint in which a new king on being inaugurated would place his foot as a sign that he would follow faithfully in the path of earlier kings. Gaelic, the language the Scots spoke, gradually spread among all the Highlanders and their name, Scots, in time covered all the people in Scotland.

Christianity also came from Ireland when Columba landed with 12 companions and established a religious centre on Iona. It was they who brought the Gospel to the Highlands. Columba travelled up the Great Glen to Inverness where he met Brude, king of the Picts, and persuaded him to give his protection to the missionaries. Proof of their success in converting the Picts is in the splendid Christian crosses that Pictish sculptors carved on the later symbol-stones in the east and north-east, which are best seen at Aberlemno in Angus. Iona's part in the art of illuminating manuscripts can be judged from the Book of Kells, taken from Iona to Ireland for safety and now in Trinity College, Dublin.

The Vikings from Scandinavia came first as raiders in search of food and treasure, raiding Iona, for example, in 806. Later they settled in Shetland, Orkney and the Western Isles, and on the mainland in Caithness, Wester Ross and Sutherland, which although in the north of Scotland was 'southern land' to the Earls of Orkney. Clues to their settlements occur in place-

names: for example, *setr* meaning a dwelling appears in Tister in Caithness and Uigshader in Skye; and *bolstathr* meaning a farm, in Scrabster in Caithness, Ullapool in Wester Ross, and Skibo and Embo in Sutherland.

Kings and the Highlands

To survive as king in those times was not easy. Duncan I, a king who was not a Highlander, was killed in battle in 1040 (not murdered in his bed as Shakespeare would have us believe) by Macbeth, the *mormaer* or effective ruler of the north. Macbeth became a strong king until he was defeated and killed by Duncan's son, Malcolm, who became king as Malcolm III.

Attempts by kings to organise Scotland through introducing Norman feudal lords, appointing sheriffs and creating towns had little effect on the Highlands up to about the year 1200. Inverness was unique in being the only burgh, a fortified place with a sheriff to represent the king, and even *his* authority did not extend far. To rule in the West Highlands required a fleet: anyone who had one could behave as if he were a king. Somerled, 'Lord of the Isles', had one, and used it to sail up the Clyde and challenge the king, Malcolm IV, but he was killed in 1164.

Other families who built advanced stone castles very early in the west were the Stewarts at Rothesay, the MacSweens with Castle Sween in Knapdale, and the Comyns at Inverlochy at the south-west end of the Great Glen. As the Comyns also held Castle Urquhart on Loch Ness at the other end of the Great Glen in 1304, and Ruthven Castle north of the Drumochter Pass (and built the first castle at Blair Atholl to the south of it), they had power right across the Highlands. Robert Bruce had either to befriend them or break them if he wanted to be king. John, 'the Red Comyn', and Bruce quarrelled and Comyn was murdered. Highlanders who fought for Robert I in Scotland's fight for independence, which was won at Bannockburn in 1314, included Mackintoshes, Campbells, MacDonalds and Stewarts.

From Somerled's son, Dougal, came the MacDougalls or sons of Dougal who, based on Dunollie Castle near Oban, were the lords of Lorn; from his son, Ranald, came the family who

Culloden 1746: the beginning of the end of the Highland clans which, with Bonnie Prince Charlie, were crushed by the Duke of Cumberland's troops in their attempt to regain the British Crown. Right: the memorial Cairn

claimed to be Lords of the Isles until about 1350; and from his grandson, Donald came the great clan of MacDonald, whose leaders were Lords of the Isles until 1492, when James IV was strong enough to bring that position to an end. He could not replace the Lord of the Isles' authority by his own, so this gave the chiefs of clans in the Highlands freedom to behave like little kings.

Chiefs as little kings

The word *clan* means the children and the chief was like an all-powerful father over them. His relatives, who held land directly from him, shared the clan surname and were the clan's chief fighting men, but men with other surnames, like the Macintyres in Clan Campbell, were in the clan because they lived on land the clan had taken. The chief was their judge with the right even to hang them. He was their commander, who could call the clan to war at any time by sending round the 'fiery cross', charred in fire and smeared in blood, and he often did this for feuds with other clans.

In one feud in 1603 Glengarry's men burned a whole congregation of Mackenzies in a church in Easter Ross. Also in 1603 the Macgregors trapped the Colquhouns in Glenfruin and slaughtered 140 of them. This surely was the time of the 'Wild Scots'. James VI outlawed every Macgregor who took part and banned the use of the name. But the Macgregors survived, usually by joining other clans. Rob Roy, who lived on cattle-thieving and protection money a century later, was a Macgregor.

Some Highland clans fought for the Marquis of Montrose in his famous year of victories, 1644–5 during the Civil War, and 50 years later, on the replacement of the Catholic King James VII by the Dutch Protestant William III, it was Highlanders

Proud memorial at Aberfeldy to the Black Watch – the earliest Highland regiment. Many others followed

again who rose and fought under 'Bonnie Dundee' at Killiecrankie in 1689. The treatment of one small clan, the MacDonalds of Glencoe, by Government soldiers who had enjoyed their hospitality for nearly a fortnight in 1692 and then put 38 of them to the sword, lives on in Highland memories as the Massacre of Glencoe.

On the accession of George of Hanover as king of Great Britain in 1714, many Highland chiefs were 'Jacobites', supporters of the exiled Stuarts, and they alone could raise men to fight. A rising in 1715 ended in a drawn battle at Sheriffmuir near Stirling and another was defeated at Glenshiel in 1719. Government troops, Redcoats under General Wade, were then stationed in forts, Fort William, Fort Augustus and Fort George, in the Highlands. They built military roads between the forts and connected them to the Lowlands, and did their best to disarm the Highlanders.

A Highland rising without French help appeared a forlorn hope by 1745 when Prince Charles Edward, grandson of James VII, arrived in the west Highlands with only seven men. Many clans would not rise but MacDonalds and Camerons raised the standards in rebellion at Glenfinnan and swept south, joined by the men of Atholl. They captured Edinburgh and proclaimed the Prince's father king, and penetrated into England as far as Derby, but found no support. After a heroic march, they returned to the Highlands, but at Culloden in 1746 their weary army was no match for the cannon, bayonets and cavalry of the British army under the Duke of Cumberland. Although 'Bonnie Prince Charlie' escaped to France, the days of the 'Wild Scots' were over.

The stamp of government

Redcoats devastated the glens with fire and sword. The Government's new laws prevented Highlanders from possessing weapons of any kind, or wearing kilt, plaid or any garment made of tartan, under pain of transportation. Even the bagpipes were banned as instruments of war.

Jacobite leaders fled and lost their estates.

Every chief lost the right to hold court and try his clansmen. Without it the clan system decayed. No longer a judge, no longer a military leader, the ex-chief was no different from any other landlord.

Highland men could still wear the tartan and fight – but only if they were in the British army! The earliest Highland regiment was the Black Watch, and among the regiments formed by 1800 were the Seaforth Highlanders, the Gordons, the Camerons, the Argylls and the Sutherland Highlanders.

Population and economic change

Traditionally Highlanders depended mainly on keeping cattle for a living, the drovers moving surplus beasts south each year to be sold at Falkirk Tryst. Good land was scarce and as population increased, the potato was a new crop which kept many of them alive, but famine struck sometimes, as it did so distressingly in 1846.

Farmers from the south would pay rents that were three times higher for the land as big sheep-farms, once the glens had been cleared. This happened on a large scale in Sutherland. In Strathnaver in 1819, for example, people had to move, as their houses were burned to make sure they did not return. Given small plots on a wild coast, they were told to make a living by fishing.

The number of Highlanders emigrating rose alarmingly by 1800 and the engineer, Thomas Telford, suggested a great public works programme – building roads, bridges, harbours and the Caledonian Canal – to create jobs and open up the Highlands. The work went on under him for twenty years, and the Canal, the roads and many of the thousand bridges are still in use today. Tourists came in but industry did not, even after the construction of railways later in the century.

After the sheep came the creation of sporting estates, especially deer forests in Inverness-shire, Skye and Wester Ross, as a cause of clearance and depopulation. The ruins of deserted settlements can be seen in empty glens but where did all the people go? Some were moved to meagre crofts on the coast, some went to industrial towns in the south, great numbers emigrated to make a new life in Canada and the United States, and later to Australia and New Zealand.

Since 1945, hydro-electricity has made houses more comfortable in the Highlands, and light industries possible. These, together with forestry and tourism have provided new jobs, whereas larger industries have been less successful. The Highlands and Islands Enterprise supports ventures which will bring work to the Highlands, a place where people are conscious of their past, but where there is room to grow.

Kilmorack power station, transforming Highland life

Mountain Landscapes

*T*he Scottish Highlands contain some of the grandest scenery in Europe, and, taken together, the landscapes of northern Scotland form one of the largest-surviving 'wilderness' areas in the Western hemisphere.

Look at a map of the British islands and a cursory glance will show that the north of Scotland is as big in area as East Anglia, the Midlands and the Home Counties put together. And yet the population is small in number, and most of it is concentrated within the towns.

That such a huge area remains almost empty and largely 'wild' (from long, deep sea-lochs penetrating far inland in the south-west, to dramatic volcanic rock cliffs on the Inner Hebrides) is remarkable when you think that northern Europe is one of the most crowded and 'developed' parts of the world. And it is the erosion, by rivers and glaciers, of the ancient rocks underlining this vast area that explains much of its appearance and character.

How the Highlands evolved

When seeing the mountains ahead, visitors approaching the Highlands from the south or south-east know immediately why the area is given this name. The boundary between the Highlands and the Lowlands of Scotland is quite definite. It runs roughly twenty miles north of Glasgow, Stirling, Perth and Montrose, continues north then west, leaving out much of Aberdeenshire and the lower lands along the Moray Firth to Inverness.

To understand the evolution of the Highland scenery we have to think in terms of four time scales. Firstly, the most ancient rocks developed between 300 million and 3000 million years ago. These metamorphic rocks, as they are known, are tough materials which have been compressed, baked and twisted, and lie beneath large areas of the Highlands. During this long phase of early geological history there were several periods of mountain building. In some ways the present mountain scenery can be regarded as the worn-down roots of a much larger, ancient mountain system. Secondly, during the last 100 million years, two very significant events occurred—a period of volcanic activity and the development of a river valley network. Thirdly, during the last two million years, there have been frequent and dramatic changes in the climate, resulting in what is generally known as the 'ice-age'. On at least 20 occasions the climate deteriorated so much that glaciers developed in the Highlands. Fourthly, the last 30,000 years have produced obvious changes in Highland landscapes, due largely to the build up and eventual disappearance of the last ice sheet to cover Scotland. Each of these phases has left its mark on the character of Highland scenery.

Rocks and structures

In the north-west mainland and in the Outer Hebrides, large areas are made up of gneiss. This rock, which probably lies under the younger rocks of much of the rest of the Highlands, was formed

Cloud-tipped Slioch from the shore of Loch Maree

over 2000 million years ago and often shows a distinctive banding, visible in various forms. In northern Lewis it underlies gently undulating areas, while in southern Lewis and western Sutherland it forms mountains.

A younger formation of metamorphic rocks occupies the south-east Highlands from Kintyre to Buchan. Called the Dalradian system, it is the main constituent of the Grampians and tends to produce smooth slopes and rounded summits. About 400 million years ago great upheavals occurred in what is known, in almost Hollywood-sounding terms, as the 'Caledonian Mountain Building Episode'. At that time great mountain chains, at least the size of the present European Alps and possibly similar in size to the Himalayas, were created by the earth's crust folding and splitting.

It was at this time that the basic 'grain' of the Highlands was established, and the Great Glen and Highland Boundary faults developed.

As the illustration shows, there are numerous outcrops of granite throughout the Highlands and Islands. Granite is most common in the Grampians, but significant outcrops also occur in Arran, Mull, Skye, Harris, Lewis and Sutherland. In most cases the granite forms rugged mountains, as in Arran and Skye, but in the Cairngorms the granite underlies smooth, flat surfaces. Most of the granites were thrust up about 500 million years ago, except for those of Skye, Mull and Arran, which were associated with volcanic activity some 60 million years ago.

Sedimentary rocks occupy only a relatively small part of the area of the Highlands and Islands. Apart from small outcrops in places such as Mull, Morven and Arran, there are two main areas: a coastal zone 10 to 20 miles wide stretching from Cape Wrath to the Sound of Sleat, and an east-coast area extending from around the shores of the Moray Firth through Caithness to Orkney. These two have very different geological characters. The western area consists of palaeozoic sandstone and limestone, which are 500 to 800 million years old, whereas the eastern area consists of Devonian sandstone and shales 350 to 400 million years old.

Contrasts

There are remarkable differences in the north-west Highlands, between the two base rocks – the Lewisian gneiss and the overlying sandstone. The Torridonian sandstone is the oldest sedimentary rock within the region and is known to be over 1600ft thick.

The best examples of these sediments are the pyramid-like mountains of Ross and Sutherland – Suilven, Quinag, and the massive, stepped mountains of the Torridon district.

The main sediments occur only to the west of one of the most distinctive structures in Scotland – the Moine Thrust. This consists of a series of faults along which great masses of rock have been moved many miles north-westwards. A major feature resulting from these thrusts are westward-facing escarpments that have been produced as a result of erosion of the rocks.

While the western area of sedimentary rocks has great mountain and valley systems, the eastern area – occupied by Devonian sediments – is characterised either by lowlands (around the shores of the Moray Firth, Caithness and most of the Orkney Islands), or by smooth, rounded hills. It is quite likely that at one time these sediments extended much further to the west, particularly in Sutherland, but were gradually removed by erosion.

The last dramatic geological event, resulting in the accumulation of solid rock in the Highlands and Islands, occurred about 60 million years ago. Major centres of volcanic activity occurred in Skye, Rum, Ardnamurchan, Mull and Arran, creating extensive flows of basalt lava. Thick accumulations of this form much of north-west Mull, Morven, and the fantastic towers and pinnacles of the Storr of Skye and the sinister fangs of the Black Cuillins. Wherever these lavas occur they form a distinctive 'stepped' landscape.

It seems likely that the Highlands were uplifted some 50 million years ago, in the form of a gently-sloping eroded surface with a general tilt to the south-east. In what is believed to have been a sub-tropical climate, a drainage system developed with the longest rivers flowing towards the east and south-east.

The basic framework of Highland scenery was established during the Tertiary Period (up to 70 million years ago), but because of the intensity of erosion during the Pleistocene Period, little is known about the details of the land's evolution during this critical period.

Metamorphic rocks

- Dalradian schist
- Moinian schist
- Lewisian gneiss

Igneous rocks

- Extrusive lava
- Intrusive lava

- - - - - - - - - - - - - *Major faults*

Sedimentary rocks

- Mesozoic sediments – sandstones, shales, limestones
- Old red sandstone
- Cambrian sediments
- Torridonian sandstone

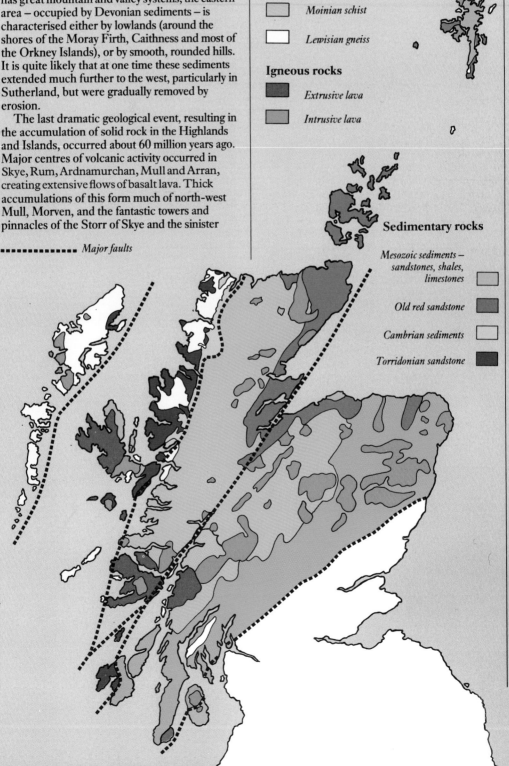

The effects of glaciation

During the last two million years the world's climate has undergone frequent and dramatic changes, which in northern latitudes have allowed glaciers and ice sheets to develop; hence the 'ice-age'. There were, in fact, numerous (maybe 20) periods, each lasting about 100,000 years when mean temperatures in Scotland during January fell by 5° to 10° C – conditions in which it would have been possible for glaciers to develop.

Events in geological history can be interpreted only from the deposits and forms these events left behind. Because glaciation produces only loosely-packed sediments, it is not surprising that, except in certain favoured localities, the deposits of earlier glaciations were destroyed by later glaciers. How many times the Scottish ice sheet built up and then retreated is not known (possibly as many as 20 times). Most of what we know about the glaciation of Scotland is based on the evidence relating to the last ice sheet which began to develop about 27,000 years ago and which finally wasted away about 10,000 years ago.

What is a glacier?

A period of glaciation starts when the snow line (the level at which the snow remains from one winter to the next), is progressively lowered. Within the Highlands and Islands, the main area of ice accumulation coincided with the zone of high ground stretching from Cape Wrath to the Firth of Clyde. These west-facing slopes had heavy falls of snow, until permanent snow banks began to form on the high ground and in the valley heads. As the climate became worse, the snow banks thickened and the snow was converted to glacier ice. In the early stages, glaciers were confined by valleys, but eventually they became so thick that even the intervening ridges were buried and an ice-cap built up. While the main ice-cap was developing in the western mountains of the mainland, other local centres of ice accumulation developed on the islands of Harris, Skye, Rum, Mull and Arran in the west, and in the Cairngorms and Monadhliath Mountains in the east. The ice-

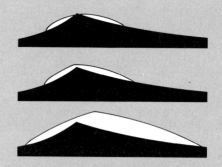

As snow banks thickened they turned to glacier ice. This eventually became so thick that intervening ridges were buried and ice caps built up

Burnside view of Ben Bhàn on the road to Applecross

moved outwards from these centres, the lines of movement being recorded by fragments of rock which can be found in the glacial deposits known as 'erratics' (pieces of rock which do not occur locally but have been transported from another area by a glacier).

The various centres of ice accumulation eventually joined to produce an ice-sheet which completely buried all the Highlands and Islands. It is unlikely that even the highest peaks stood above the surface of the ice, because the highest parts of the ice probably reached altitudes of about 5000ft. Individual ice-streams within the ice-sheet were up to 3000ft thick and probably moved at rates of between 30 and 600ft per year. This

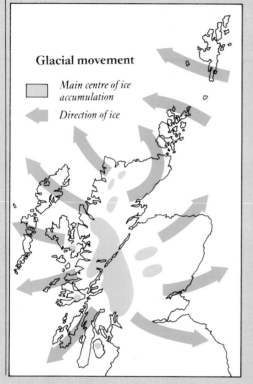

Glacial movement

Main centre of ice accumulation

Direction of ice

ice-sheet reached its maximum extent about 18,000 years ago and by 13,000 years ago had disappeared. Then, about 11,000 years ago, a sharp deterioration of climate allowed the build up of glaciers in the western Highlands and in other areas of high ground.

Glacier ice itself is not very hard but, as nearly all glaciers pick up fragments of rock in their lower layers, the underside is rather like a piece of sandpaper. As the glaciers move forward under the force of gravity, they erode and scoop out the rock surfaces of the valley heads over which they pass, to produce 'armchair' hollows known as cirques or corries. As ice moves, the sides of the valleys tend to be straightened and steepened, and the floors deepened. A typical glaciated valley is trough-like with straight, steep sides and with a basin gouged out of its floor. Some of these ice-gouged basins are very deep: Loch Morar 1017ft, Loch Ness 754ft and Loch Lomond 623ft, for example.

As they grind along, glaciers carry the eroded material over and within the ice and re-deposit it. When the ice melts, the transported material is released to form a characteristically unsorted debris and boulder clay called till. These deposits are to be found extensively in the Highlands and Islands and are an important surface material on the lower slopes of even the highest areas. The amount of debris is sometimes so great that the glacier ice becomes completely buried with boulders, gravel, sand and clay. Eventually the ice beneath the material melts and a series of hills 10 to 50ft high is produced. These morainic mounds give a wild appearance to the floor of many a Highland glen.

Outlook: warmer and wetter

When the glaciers of the Highlands began to melt, vast quantities of water were released. The lower ends of some valleys remained blocked by ice while the upper ends were ice free. This allowed large, deep lakes to develop with glacier ice acting

The Pass of the Cattle looking toward Loch Kishorn

as a dam. The most famous example within the Highlands was in Glen Roy (north of Fort William), where the lake lasted sufficiently long for shorelines to develop along the valley side.

The obvious routes for most of the meltwaters to follow during the retreat of the glaciers were the valley floors. The rivers we now see in the Highland glens increased in volume many times during the summer melt periods. These swollen rivers deposited large quantities of boulders, gravel and sand on the valley floor, and subsequently the rivers began to cut into these deposits to produce the fine river terraces seen in many Highland glens.

As the glaciers began to retreat from the Highlands during the last glaciation, the land was still so depressed by the weight of the ice that the

There may be snow on distant peaks, but Kilchurn Castle and Loch Awe lie warm in the autumn sunshine

sea level, astonishingly, was relatively higher than it is today. Around many parts of the Highland coastline, evidence of this phenomenon can be seen by the remains of marine platforms, cliff lines and raised beaches.

The age of ice came to an end some 10,000 years ago, and with the improving climate, the Highlands were rapidly colonised by oak, birch and pine. The landscape encountered by the earliest humans (about 8000 years ago) was very different from that of today. In the following centuries man was to transform the Highlands from forest to moorland, but that is another story . . .

Wilderness Wildlife

So far as we know, all the wild plant and animal life in the Highlands have colonised the area during the past 15,000 years. The bare debris of gravel left behind after the ice age was first clothed with vegetation characteristic of the Scandinavian tundra – mosses, scrubby willows and dwarf birches and hardy plants, such as heather and crowberry. In time, a taller forest of birch and juniper developed, and the trees of more temperate climates, such as Scots pine, oak, hazel, alder and ash, gradually spread in from the lowlands as the land mellowed under the warm post-glacial sun. When man first appeared as a hunter-gatherer in the Highlands, about 8000 years ago, all except the highest and wettest land may have been covered by trees. The 'Caledonian Forest' of Scots pine covered much of the drier soils of the eastern Highlands. In the milder, more humid climate of the west, oak dominated the lower slopes but in the harsher peatland landscape of the far north, woodland may have been confined to nooks of deep soil in the coastal glens. Sutherland and Caithness probably never supported much more than an open scrub of birch, juniper and willow.

Disappearing wildlife

We have lost much of the wildlife of those ancient forests. Lynx, bear, elk and wild cattle disappeared long ago, but wild reindeer survived in the far north until the 12th century and beaver until the 16th, while the last Highland wolf perished as recently as 1743. The forests themselves were long protected by their remoteness. But the 'taming' of the Highlands during the 18th century began a period of over-exploitation with profound results to the scenery and wildlife. The smelting industry of the west coast converted many of the finest oaks to charcoal while the tallest pines of the east were felled and sent down river to the timber markets. There was little respite for young trees to replace their sires, for animals were put into the woods to graze while flockmasters deliberately burned woods to extend their sheep ranges. Stocking the hills with red deer for the Victorian sportsman further limited the regeneration of the natural woods, and were it not for plantings by enlightened owners to replace them, the hills would be bare indeed. The loss of the Caledon Forest caused widespread soil erosion and improverishment, particularly in the west, and the resultant bare, boney landscape of today has often been called a 'wet desert' in consequence. It presents a spectacle of stark beauty to the visitor, but it is a haunted landscape for it once contained both trees and men.

Woodland – old and new

Today's Highlands contain more woodland than at any time since the 18th century, but most of this consists of young plantations of imported conifers, monotonous to look at and even more monotonous to walk through. Naturalists seek out the fragments of older, more natural woods which are,

fortunately, still quite extensive in certain parts of the Highlands. The most famous of these are the old pine-woods, whose sonorous names – Rannoch, Rothiemurchus, Ballochbuie, Abernethy and Glen Affric – conjure up images of primaeval mossy groves, carpeted with blaeberry, in which crested tits forage among the juniper and capercaillies swell and strut like ancestral turkey-cocks. There *are* such places in the Highlands but they have to be sought; the visitor must abandon his car and be prepared to walk several miles, but the rewards can be great. Eagles still nest on trees in some of the eastern pinewoods and buzzards are quite frequent. The Scottish crossbill, a colourful, parrot-like finch whose curiously shaped bill is

A chequered skipper at rest. Normally its quick, darting flight makes it a difficult butterfly to observe

designed to extract seed from pine cones, is found nowhere else in the world. In the boggy clearings in some of the Speyside pinewoods, greenshank nest among the heather. And, the lucky visitor will catch a glimpse of a wildcat or even a pine marten, for these beautiful mammals have increased their range since the days when the gin-trap brought them to the brink of extinction in Scotland.

The Highlands contain types of other 'wild wood' which probably resemble the original forest quite closely. Rassal Ashwood, in Ross, is a tangle of cankered old trees, twisting over mossy blocks of limestone. In the spring, it rings to the song of warbler, tit, robin and thrush, a green oasis of bustle in the wind-swept moor. Morrone Birkwood, near Braemar, is one of our few surviving Alpine woods, where mountain flowers, spangling the grass beneath the miniature birch trees, recall the remote Highland spring which followed the age of ice. The oakwoods of the west coast, on the shores of Loch Sunart and the Sound of Jura, are lush and humid compared with woods further east. Their floors are carpeted with ferns and herb-rich grassland in which the abundant butterflies include the beautiful pearl-bordered fritillary and the rare chequered skipper. But the features which place these woods in international renown are their mosses and lichens which plaster the bark and festoon the branches with their feathery or seaweed-like growths.

Going up

But as a visitor to the Highlands you will seek not the woods but the hills. On the way to the high tops, you will pass through several zones of moorland vegetation – heather, mat-grass, deer-grass, each punctuated by boggy runnels and depressions spotted with the white flowers of cloudberry, the mountain bramble, and the red and green cushions of Sphagnum moss. You will hear the sounds of the hill – the sibilant call of the meadow pipit, the melancholy pipe of the golden plover and, above all, the bubbling cry of the curlew. In the east, these moorland areas are dominated by heather, which forms a glorious flowering mantle of royal purple in August, before assuming its mellow autumn colours. In the spring, many heather moors will be striped with small burned patches. Burning is the traditional way of maintaining the moor, for heather can grow faster than animals can graze it and, if left unmanaged, it becomes dry and 'leggy'. Fire produces a young, more nutritious sward, which can support higher densities of red grouse and grazing animals.

The red grouse is the most familiar bird of the heather moors and plays an important part in the economy of Highland estates. The size of the burned patch is designed to coincide with the territory of a cock bird and a well-maintained moor will contain many more nesting pairs than one which has been allowed to become run down and neglected. Grouse moors are also the best places to see mountain hares, which are more thick-set than their lowland relative, with bigger heads and shorter ears. In the summer, the

Golden eagle and chick in their remote mountain eyrie

One of the lush and humid oak woodlands in Argyll

Pearl-bordered fritillary: a mainly woodland butterfly with a rapid flight

mountain hare has a coat of brownish-grey fur, but it moults in the autumn to produce its snow-white raiment. A hare looks absurdly conspicuous on the brown hillside in years when the snow melts early, however.

On the wing

Flying insects are always a feature of the Scottish moors although those which press their attentions most persistently are the clegs and midges which plague the boggy districts of the north and west. Altogether more attractive are the two mountain butterflies, the mountain ringlet and the large heath which fly – or are blown – over bare hillsides, sometimes accompanied by large day-flying moths such as the emperor, Scotland's only wild silk-moth, and the northern eggar. Many Highland moths have a life-cycle of two years or more, perhaps an insurance against the fickle Highland summer. One particularly beautiful moth, the Kentish glory (which, despite its name, is confined to the Highlands) can remain in its cocoon for up to seven years.

Most visitors to the Scottish moors will see red deer. The best season is autumn when the stags become fiercely territorial and the browning hills echo to their eerie roars. Deer come to lower ground in the winter to shelter in their ancestral habitat, the wooded glens. Hungry deer will raid gardens and crop fields in winter and west coast animals will even eat seaweed. The hinds wander less far than stags, and retire in the spring to calve in remote corries. The Highland red deer are free-ranging wild animals, although most of them are descended from introduced European stock. On lower ground, some estates now farm deer for venison within large fenced paddocks. But the wild deer will be a valuable asset to the Highland estate so long as there are people who are prepared to pay to stalk them.

Mountain flowers

Eventually we reach the heady air of the high tops. Beautiful, and perhaps unfamiliar, flowers will soon catch the eye. The mountain environment poses many problems for wild flowers. They must endure cold and high winds, scant or infertile soil, a short growing season, heavy rain and, conversely, severe drought: in a typical Highland summer, a plant may be frosted one day and exposed to drying winds the next. Consequently some flowers grow in tight rosettes or mats, and this growth habit, which combines small leathery leaves with large, colourful flowers, gives us some of our most attractive species. In the Cairngorms, the pink stars of moss campion and trailing azalea are among the few bright colours in the stony desert of the plateau. Other plants seek sheltered pockets of deep soil in the gullies and ledges of

Fearsomely aggressive, night-hunting wildcats are not all bad – they keep down the number of small animals that damage trees

steep cliffs. Such places have much in common with the dark, moist floor of rocky woodlands, and, indeed, woodland flowers like red campion and wood sorrel are commonly found high up on the mountains. Curiously enough, the now ubiquitous rosebay willow-herb originated as a plant of mountain cliffs and was once regarded as a rarity. Frost-sensitive mountain ferns grow in places covered by snow until late in the season, for beneath the snow the plants are protected from wind and extreme cold.

Some mountains possess a much richer flora than others. Hills like Ben Lawers in Perthshire and Caenlochan in Angus are justifiably famous as 'botanical Meccas' although there are many other less-famous hills which are almost as rewarding. Ben Lawers is composed of lime-rich rocks which weather to form deep, fertile soils, and support grass rather than heather. It therefore appears from a distance as a green hill, contrasting strongly with nearby Schiehallion and the hills of Rannoch whose granites and quartzites form poorer soils and whose flanks are clad with heather. The hanging rock gardens of Ben Lawers are resplendent with the jewel-like flowers of mountain saxifrages, gentians, forget-me-nots, speedwells and mouse-ears. In the past, some of their admirers sought these plants with trowels and sacks. Mountain flowers include some of our rarest species and should be left in their magnificent setting for everyone to enjoy.

High flyers

Only a small number of birds are hardy enough to nest on the high tops and, of these, the ptarmigan

Branches everywhere: the magnificent red deer stag (here about 7 years old) is Britain's largest wild animal, standing 4 ft high at the shoulder

is the most conspic-uous. There are said to be only two roads in the Highlands which pass through ptarmigan territory. In the spring, the dis-playing cock birds soar upwards and descend on rapidly beating wings, giv-ing vent to belch-like croaks. They are unusually 'tame' birds, confident in their hostile domain, and will usually allow the visitor to approach within a few yards; they even seem at home on crowded ski-slopes. Much rarer than the ptarmigan is the dotterel, a beautiful arctic plover which visits the high tops in summer. The dotterel's nesting behaviour is unusual in that it is the cock which incubates the eggs while the hen defends the territory. In the Cairngorms you may also hear the sweet song of the snow bunting. Every summer, a few of these attractive finches remain to nest among the boulder fields of the high plateau, which so resembles their main breeding grounds in the arctic tundra. But more often they are seen in flocks, aptly known as 'snowflakes', in the early spring, feeding on ski-resort crumbs like suburban sparrows before their long journey north.

Rose bay willow-herb entwined with bindweed

Highland fish

The waters of Highland rivers and lochs are cold and clear. Salmon 'run' up fast-flowing rivers like the Dee and Spey to their spawning grounds in the gravel reaches in the heart of the Highlands. Trout, on the other hand, are common in most lochs and streams. Some of the deep mountain lochs also contain char, a beautiful red and black relative of the trout, whose isolated breeding pools have nurtured a large number of different races. Accompanying the char in some of these cold, remote places is the 'ferox' trout, a heavy variety with large black spots against a background of deep gold. The dark, mysterious freshwaters of the Highlands have attracted their share of legend; the monster, which may or may not inhabit Loch Ness, has his counterpart in the 'kelpies' who dwell in the allegedly bottomless 'pots' of deep rivers. They take the form of aquatic horses, oxen or beings of more devilish appearance, with horns and eyes like hot coals.

Every Highland river eventually reaches the sea, and the west coast, with its gaunt, craggy headlands, its sweet, secluded sea lochs thronged with marine life, and its sand and shingle strands is a paradise for the naturalist. On the north coast, blown sand may support buttercups, clover, eyebrights, stork's-bills and wild pansies in a springy herbal carpet known as machair. At Durness in Sutherland, plants normally found on mountains, such as mountain avens and bearberry, spill over on to the dunes in a spectacle of wild colour. These are among the last places on the mainland where one can regularly hear (but seldom see) corncrakes among the scented fields.

Salmon can leap falls 11ft high, taking off at 20mph

Island colonies

The most spectacular bird colonies are to be found on the off-shore islands. Handa, near the Sutherland coast, has steep cliffs with horizontal ledges crowded with thousands of guillemots, razorbills, kittiwakes and fulmars. The mountainous island of Rum, often said to look from a distance like a basket of eggs, possesses a huge colony of Manx shearwaters which nest in burrows in the soft soils of the mountainsides. Shearwaters are ocean birds which come to land only at night. It is an unforgettable experience to hear the raucous screams of the unseen birds as they circle about your head and land with a soft 'flump' before scurrying off into the darkness.

Islay is another rewarding island. The steep cliffs of the Mull of Oa are the Scottish home of the chough (pronounced 'chuff') perhaps the most attractive and certainly the rarest of the crow family, and also one of the world's strongholds for the rare Greenland races of white-fronted and barnacle goose.

The future

What of the future of Highland wildlife? Some indications are encouraging, others less so. Many of the finest remaining wild places are protected as nature reserves by Scottish Natural Heritage, the Royal Society for the Protection of Birds and the Scottish Wildlife Trust. Some of the most spectacular animals, such as grey seal, red squirrel and wild cat are more widespread and numerous today than they were at the turn of the century. The osprey has returned to Scotland and so too, with a little help from the Nature Conservancy, has the magnificent white-tailed

Fulmars soar effortlessly on long, narrow wings

eagle. Moral attitudes have changed for the better: few of us nowadays would care to shoot a rare falcon or fill a hamper with rare mountain ferns. Depite some unfortunate local developments, modern tourism has not seriously harmed Highland wildlife, and there is every reason, given sensible planning policies, to suppose that the two are compatible.

On the debit side, an increasing proportion of the Highlands is passing out of the hands of the traditional families and clans and into those of institutions and financiers whose motives are primarily one of profit. One such effect has been the afforestation of peat bogs, hardly suitable for trees but of great importance for breeding birds, in the flow country of Sutherland and Caithness. Ugly, bulldozed tracks, designed mainly to save industrialist stalkers the use of their legs, have scarred many a Highland fastness, while the native woodlands are steadily dwindling in extent through poor management and the over-grazing of deer, cattle and sheep. A still more insidious menace is acid rain, a looming threat to soils, to trees, to fish and, above all, to the unique lichen flora of the western woods.

Problems such as those have no simple solution. But in many ways, the visitor who wishes to see Highland wildlife has never had it so good. Information centres will have details of the many long-distance footpaths, nature trails and areas of special interest which are available for the traveller. The basic rules are: leave your car behind, take sensible precautions against bad weather and rough ground, and treat what you find with respect. The Scottish Highlands is one of the last wildernesses of Europe; it has enriched the spirit of many an earlier traveller; let it do the same for you.

Highlands by the Sea

*S*uch is the splendour of its moorland and mountain, loch and glen that, in terms of natural beauty, Scotland is comparable with any part of the world. So familiar are these attractions, however, that there is one important feature that is overlooked – the country's Highland seaside. Many people head from Britain's south coast or make the long haul abroad every year to be beside the seaside, but how many of them are aware of the number of attractive beaches in the north of Scotland?

Skye's the limit

The rugged coastline to the west separates the mainland from the Isle of Skye, where the magnificent Cuillin Hills and majestic mountains contrast sharply with the sandy beaches nestling beneath them.

The beaches at Glen Brittle and

The small Buchan fishing village of Pennan, on a rocky coastal stretch overlooked by Pennan Head

Camasunary are in an area from which mountain rescue operations are often co-ordinated. Camasunary is best reached via Elgol, following a rough track, best suited to Land Rovers or similar four-wheel-drive vehicles. Across the waters of Loch Scavaig and Loch Slapin lies the safe and sandy beach at Tarskavaig, in the picturesque parish of Sleat. The main centre of Skye is Portree, which is about 34 miles from the ferry terminal at Kyle of Lochalsh. This is a pleasant, bustling village, which has a wide range of shops and hotels, as well as bed and breakfast accommodation.

Across the blustery Minch, in lovely Wester Ross, the Gairloch peninsula boasts several beaches, all within a relatively short distance of one another. For many people Wester Ross holds particular charm. The traditional way of life seems to remain unaffected by time, in contrast with other areas which have played host to high-wage industries such as oil-platform construction yards.

Passing by Badachro, on Loch Gairloch, leads to Red Point beach. This is a delightful place, sheltered from the hustle and bustle of other areas because the road reaches a dead end here. The Badachro peninsula is very popular with holidaymakers, not least because of the seclusion it offers. There is easy access to Gairloch, which offers excellent facilities for sailing. Every summer, there is a regatta which attracts many entries from locals and visitors alike.

Award-winning museum

There is a museum at Gairloch giving a fascinating insight into the area's way of life through the ages. It is run by the Gairloch Heritage Society and has won several awards. Gairloch has a good selection of accommodation of all types and has its own fine sandy beach, with a magnificent view towards the north end of Skye.

Travelling north from Gairloch, do not miss the chance to explore the famous Inverewe Gardens near Poolewe. Established by Osgood Mackenzie over 100 years ago and now owned by the National Trust for Scotland, the gardens have plants from many distant parts of the world.

Near Laide, there is a splendid beach at Mellon Udrigle, sheltered and secluded on the shores of Gruinard Bay and with a wonderful view to the mountains of Sutherland. This is another tiny village, its inhabitants making a living off the land.

There is a superb stretch of sand by the main road at the head of Gruinard Bay, which attracts many people each summer. Gruinard Island, in the bay, was contaminated by anthrax spores in 1942 during germ warfare experiments and has only recently been declared safe again.

Farther north in Wester Ross, there are more beaches in the Coigach area, and at Achiltibuie, a quiet place offering tranquillity to those who seek it. An especially interesting feature here is the Hydroponicum, where crops including bananas, strawberries, figs and vines are grown without soil. It is open to visitors in the summer. From Achiltibuie you can visit the lovely Summer Isles.

The north-west coastline of Skye – the Misty Isle

Into Sutherland

Crossing into the county of Sutherland, another excellent beach can be found at Clachtoll, near Lochinver. The new Kylesku Bridge leads to Scourie, also a popular holiday area. Tarbet has a beach, and offshore here is the RSPB reserve of Handa Island, a Mecca for ornithologists.

Kinlochbervie, a bustling village, is destined to be one of the main fisheries centres in the Highlands in the years ahead. Near here are more fine beaches at Oldshoremore, Sheigra, and perhaps the best of all, glorious Sandwood Bay, which can only be reached by a long walk.

Scotland's north coast has much to offer – superb cliff scenery, quiet coves and splendid beaches. Durness has the craft centre at Balnakiel, the dramatic Smoo Cave, and beaches at Sango Bay. There are stretches of sand all around the Kyle of Tongue – crossed by a causeway – and a fine beach at Torrisdale Bay, near Bettyhill, before you enter Caithness.

Here is some of the best coastline in Britain. The lighthouse at Strathy Point is well worth a visit for its superb views, then both Strathy Bay and Melvich Bay have excellent sand, as does Sandside Bay, a couple of miles west of Dounreay, where the nuclear energy research establishment has a visitor centre that offers a very different kind of experience.

Thurso is the largest town of Caithness, swelled in recent years by people coming to work at Dounreay, and it has all the facilities you would expect. From Scrabster, on Thurso Bay, the ferry leaves for Orkney. A few miles east is the wonderful sweep of sand at Dunnet Bay, comparable with the finest beaches anywhere – except perhaps for the temperature of the water! This area is renowned for its onshore waves, and windsurfing championships are regularly held here.

Dunnet Head, the most northerly point on the British mainland, should not be missed, then it's on past the Castle of Mey, holiday home of the Queen Mother, to John o'Groats – and, if you are wise, a couple more miles to Duncansby Head, where a short walk enables you to see the magnificent stacks and the dramatic Sclaites Geo, an inlet cut deeply into the coast by the sea.

North of Wick is another extensive stretch of sand round Sinclair's Bay. On its south side are the twin ruined castles of Sinclair and Girnigoe. Farther south, the old crofting village at Badbea has been recreated as a visitor attraction, and Helmsdale boasts another award-winning museum, called Timespan.

Brora, Golspie and in particular Dornoch all have fine beaches – and golf courses to match them! Dornoch also has its historic 13th-century cathedral, and fine views over the Dornoch Firth. The small village of Embo nearby has another beach but is better known for Granny's Hielan' Hame, where *ceilidhs* with music and dancing are regularly held.

Return to Ross

Back into Ross and Cromarty – and there is no shortage of beaches in Easter Ross: Tain, Portmahomack, Hilton, Inver, Balintore and Shandwick, all quite close to one another. Tain, the biggest of these, is an ancient royal burgh with full shopping and accommodation facilities, as well as a golf course. Easter Ross is primarily a farming community and nowadays the only large-scale heavy industry is the oil-platform construction yard at Nigg Bay, on the shores of Cromarty Firth. It is rolling fertile land, in total contrast to Wester Ross with its rugged scenery.

The Black Isle area is fertile farming land, too. This is not an island at all, but a peninsula, with new bridges both north and south built within recent years, making it an excellent centre with easy access to the main roads. It has beaches at Rosemarkie and Fortrose, with a golf course and a caravan site

Fishing nets drying at Cruden Bay – a resort noted for its fine sand and championship golf course

nearby.

On the other side of the Moray Firth, there is a very good beach for caravanners at Nairn, which is a bustling town offering good hotels and accommodation.

Farther along to the east, there is a prominent beach at Findhorn, close to the RAF station at Kinloss. This goes along to Burghead and then there is a long beach at Lossiemouth, which is again in the shadow of an RAF station. In Banff and Buchan district, there is a beach at Sandend (between Portsoy and Cullen); with a small beach and caves at Cullykhan, between Gardenstown and Pennan. There are also beaches at Fraserburgh and Peterhead, both towns which grew out of the fishing industry.

Capital beaches

South of Peterhead, Cruden Bay has splendid sands, a championship golf course, and the ruins of Slains Castle, said to have inspired Bram Stoker to write *Dracula*. The Bullers of Buchan seacliffs are noted for their magnificent birdlife.

Finally, there is a glorious stretch of sand running all the way from Newburgh to Aberdeen – a distance of 10 miles. At Sands of Forvie, on the Ythan estuary near Newburgh, another bird reserve can be visited.

At the southern end of this long curve of sand, towards Aberdeen, you will find cafés, discos and amusement arcades, in what is said to be the largest such site in Scotland. For those seeking the quiet life, however, the rest of the beach remains unspoilt, and you can walk for miles enjoying the sea air, the birds and the views, as you can in so many places around the Highland coast.

As for Aberdeen itself . . . well, it may be one of the oil capitals of the world, but people who know the city maintain that it has retained its character. Its docks, rivers and beaches will always give it the feel of a city by the sea.

The Games

Athletic competitions have a long history in Scotland. There is a tradition that King Malcolm III, as long ago as the 11th century, held a contest on the Braes of Mar to find his fastest runners and toughest fighting men.

The Braemar Gathering, under royal patronage since the days of Queen Victoria, is one of the highlights of the Highland year. But there are dozens of other Games, large and small, all over the Highlands in the summer months. Dates and venues are available from tourist information centres.

Community affairs

In many parts of Scotland the gatherings had their beginnings in purely social events, such as weddings, where the celebrations would include challenges of one type or another, and where the whole community would become involved. A lot of the events seen today developed from the simple amusements of local workers. High- and long-jumping and running events (including hill races) could be carried out with the minimum of equipment, but as a change from slaving over a hot anvil,

Tossing the caber at the Cowal Highland Gathering, Dunoon

blacksmiths would see how far they could throw their hammers or iron weights. Well-rounded stones, suitable for 'putting' were retrieved from rivers. Forest workers used a branch-stripped tree trunk (*cabar* in Gaelic) for their own trial of strength and skill.

'Ye casting of ye bar', as tossing the caber was once known, is perhaps the most remarkable and thrilling of all the events. The straight, heavy pine trunk (the Braemar caber is almost 20ft long and weighs 132lb) is grasped vertically in the competitor's cupped hands at its smaller end. The object is to heave the tapering caber with a mighty jerk on to its thicker end so that it describes a semi-circle and lands in as near a straight line as possible from the competitor. It is an art calling not only for extraordinary strength, but also canny balance and timing.

Unsung heroes

Today, many of the athletes are professionals and for this reason the impressive performances do not find their way into the record books. This is especially true of track events; times set by competitors in sprint events have often approached Olympic standards. Ricky Dunbar, an Edinburgh sprinter, for example, dashed off 100 yards in 9.6 seconds, and the 100 metres has been clocked in 11.0 seconds. In the heavy events, former Olympian Geoff Capes has become a great favourite in recent years.

Competitors in light events wear conventional running kit but this was not always so. Who of the spectators watching a certain Peter Cameron will forget the day this daring young man achieved a high jump of 5ft 7in *wearing a kilt*?

More than muscle

But Highland Gatherings have always been more than just an opportunity to display physical fitness. Piping and dancing – important aspects of the martial tradition – were also popular. So much so that at various times laws were passed to prohibit them – archery and swordplay were considered of more importance in the interest of national defence. In the 1870s, however (following the lifting of the ban on the wearing of the tartan, imposed by the victorious British after the defeat of the Jacobite cause, many people thought it important to encourage these aspects of Scottish culture. Thus they once again became a feature of the Games.

The *piobaireachd* (pronounced peebroch) is the centuries-old classical music of the bagpipes, and prizes in piping are highly coveted. As well as slow-time strathspeys and jaunty jigs and reels, marches are also represented, for the pipes were considered an instrument of war as well as peace.

Anyone holidaymaking in the Highlands from June to September should try to attend at least one of the colourful and thrilling Games – among the most soul-stirring and picturesque sights in the world – with their uniquely Scottish, indeed Highland, individuality.

Spreading Their Wings

A look at how the Highlands and Islands Development Board and its successor, Highlands and Islands Enterprise, aim to encourage investment and employment in the area.

The Highlands and Islands Development Board (HIDB) was set up by the government in 1965. Its brief was 'to assist the people of the area to improve their economic and social conditions, and to enable the area to play a more effective part in the economic and social development of the nation.' But why was a development board necessary in an area whose greatest asset, it could be argued, was its very lack of development? In order to understand that, we have to go back 250 years.

The HIDB's area of operations (now taken over by HIE) stretches from Kintyre up to Shetland, and from Morayshire over to the Outer Hebrides. It encompasses one-sixth of the entire land mass of Britain, but has a population of only about 370,000 (a number which is now slowly increasing, from a low of 320,000 in 1961). This equates to the joint population of the London boroughs of Camden and Islington. Such a sparse population will always find it difficult to generate wealth and improve living standards without assistance.

The Highlands were not always so empty: walk through any glen and you will see the remains of settlements long since vanished, and for every one you see there were ten others. The pivotal year was 1746, when the last Jacobite Rising ended in defeat and debacle at Culloden. Bonnie Prince Charlie, after incredible adventures, escaped to France, never to return, and the Highlanders who had supported him were hunted and outlawed.

Over the following 150 years, the 'Clearances' took hundreds of thousands of people from the land and shipped them, willingly or not, to the new colonies of the USA, Canada and later Australia and New Zealand. The clan system was broken, the remnant population were forced into coastal settlements, and vast areas of the Highlands became sheep-runs or sporting estates.

Towards the end of the 19th century, under great pressure, the government of the time reluctantly enacted legislation which enabled individuals to rent smallholdings on modest terms in perpetuity. This is the crofting system, something unique to the Highlands. A croft is a piece of land (not, as often erroneously thought, a house) ranging from one acre up to perhaps 30 acres. Grouped together, they become a crofting township, which often has access to larger areas for communal grazing.

It is a way of life rather than a livelihood, though greatly cherished and defended passionately – and you will find crofters working part of the time as fishermen, garage mechanics, drivers and many other things.

Every Scottish clan has its own colourful tartan, each one different in some respect from all the others

Bed and breakfast makes an important contribution, as it does all over the Highlands. The Scottish Crofters Union, established only in 1985, has quickly become a highly effective lobbying body, and already has over 4,000 members. One of the organisations it regularly lobbied – with favourable results – was HIDB.

Help at hand
Many people saw HIDB as providing the answer to all the ills of the Highlands when it was set up. It never could do that, but it has offered regular and increasing support over a vast range of economic, social and cultural activities. In its last year of operation, 1990–91, it had a budget of £47 million, and directly assisted nearly 1,500 businesses or communities to the tune of £16 million. In addition, over £6 million went to projects such as support for area tourist boards, business advisory services and training, and £7 million was spent on marketing. In the ten years from 1981 to 1990, approximately

20,000 jobs were created and a further 5,500 safeguarded as a result of Board assistance.

The projects and activities receiving HIDB support cover an extraordinary range – from underwriting travel costs for a soccer team to fly to the Outer Hebrides, to assisting theatre and music groups to visit outlying communities, to funding business and tourism ventures of every kind. The list of research projects for 1990 alone runs to over 150 subjects, from a three-year evaluation of the Highland mule to a feasibility study for a visitor centre at the famous Callanish standing stones site on Lewis. Support was also given to a year-long artistic programme in the Highlands, called HI-Light.

Farms, fish and people

The land and the sea have always been deeply interwoven components of Highland life. Although agriculture now provides employment for only about 9,000 people on a full-time equivalent basis, it is still a major activity covering very substantial areas of land. The ocean, too, has long supplied both food and work. Here, things have changed dramatically in the past 20–30 years, and the HIDB has been a major player in the drama.

The modern story began 200 years ago when, in an effort to help struggling communities on the coast, the British Fisheries Society built planned villages at a number of sites, including Tobermory, on the island of Mull, and Ullapool in Wester Ross. Fishing continued to develop through the 19th and early 20th centuries, but in recent years, new technology led to serious overfishing of inner waters and a consequent decline in the industry.

The major fishing ports are now Aberdeen, Fraserburgh and Peterhead in the north-east and Kinlochbervie in the far north-west. Fleets still operate from Wick, Oban and other ports, but on a much reduced level, while at Ullapool you will often see factory ships – the 'klondykers' – from Eastern Europe or the Soviet Union waiting offshore to load up with fish for processing. The numbers employed full-time in sea fishing have declined; but at the same time, a new industry arose at a phenomenally rapid rate.

This was fish farming, in which large tanks are suspended in lochs and fish are bred in controlled conditions. Salmon is still the principal harvest but trout, halibut and other fish are also being farmed successfully, and shellfish farming is widespread. From a small, low-key beginning in the 1970s, fish farming grew rapidly, and by 1988 there were 250 fish farms and 175 shellfish farms employing over 1,600 full-time staff. It is now proving impossible to sustain this growth, which is hardly surprising, and there has been increasing concern expressed over the environmental impact of fish farming. The industry looks set for a period of rationalisation but, in employment terms, it can be counted a considerable success, and HIDB had much to do with that.

Forestry has also spread widely over the Highlands. There has been a marked shift away from the state-run Forestry Commission to planting by private companies, and again

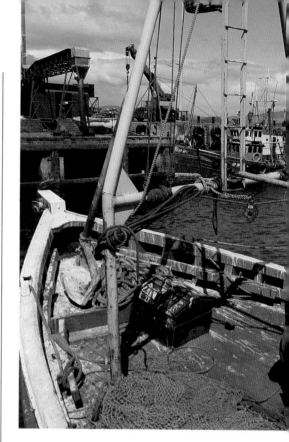

Fisherman's-eye view of the busy harbour at mallaig

there have been fierce environmental battles, most notably in the 'Flow Country' of Caithness and Sutherland, but the industry still employs around 3,000 men on site and a further 500 or so in processing, sawmills, and so on. Planting has slowed since the 1988 Budget cut the amount of grant available.

A Highland welcome

Tourism is vitally important to the Highlands. The latest figures indicate an estimated 3.5 million visitors coming to this most lovely part of Britain in 1990, and bringing an economic benefit of £400 million with them – over £1,000 per head of population in the area.

There is always a danger of 'killing the golden goose', but so far, with a few exceptions, tourism has avoided the worst excesses of rampant commercialism in the Highlands, and has developed largely in tune with the environment which the visitors come to see and savour. There is even talk now (1991) of the Aviemore Centre, which many have felt to be starkly unsuited to its setting, being largely redeveloped on 'greener' lines with new, lower buildings.

Much HIDB money went into tourism, either in supporting new development, upgrading existing accommodation, administering the area's tourist boards, or encouraging new facilities and visitor attractions. Accommodation is split almost equally between the three principal categories with roughly 1,100 hotels and guest houses, 1,500 self-catering units, and 1,400 bed and breakfast establishments.

It is at the latter that many people feel they receive the truest Highland welcome. In a surprising number of cases, the householders stumbled into B&B almost by accident, but having ventured in, they find it enjoyable and a useful addition to the budget. In return, the

Gairloch fishing fleet about to weigh anchor. In contrast (left), Aberdeen's Victoria Docks in 1885

visitor gets the benefit of local knowledge and a genuinely homely welcome, and the facilities are of a very high standard. The same goes for the guest houses and hotels, many of which started as changehouses on coaching routes or as lodges for sportsmen carrying rod and gun. So the message is – don't be afraid to be adventurous. You'll be delighted at what you find in the smaller establishments and those off the beaten track.

The scenery is undoubtedly the top attraction in the Highlands and Islands. There is a long and fascinating history here too, and its story is told, not just in those buildings that have survived the centuries, but innovatively and interestingly in a wide range of museums and other visitor attractions.

In the area covered by this guide, you can range from a museum at Bettyhill telling the sad story of the Clearances to one portraying farming life, at Aden Country Park in Buchan, and on to the thatched cottage in Cromarty where the pioneer geologist Hugh Miller spent much of his life. Timespan at Helmsdale uses modern techniques to tell the long story of human life in the area, and at Landmark, Carrbridge, you can take a treetop trail to learn about the natural history and wildlife of

Strathspey and the Cairngorms.

There are many more examples, and a selection is listed in the Fact File on pages 72–76. As well as exhibitions and museums, the area has a magnificent array of craft shops, with items of outstanding quality on show and for sale. Whether your taste is for jewellery, pottery, clothing or woodwork you will not be disappointed. The development of the craft industry was again greatly helped by HIDB. The Made in Scotland marketing group pulls many of the diverse strands together, and the annual craft fair at Aviemore in the autumn is attended by buyers and press from many countries.

Looking ahead
In April 1991, HIDB became HIE – Highlands and Islands Enterprise, with a new logo and a new motto, *Spread Your Wings in the Highlands and Islands.* HIE takes over most of HIDB's former role and adds to it the important training function previously handled by a separate agency.

One other major difference is that enterprise development will now be in the hands of 10 Local Enterprise Companies, with HIE overseeing and guiding policy. It is hoped that this will make help more accessible, in that wherever you are, you have your own LEC to turn to, rather than a branch office of a board based in Inverness. The 10 companies will cover: Shetland, Orkney, The Western Isles, Caithness & Sutherland, Ross & Cromarty, Skye & Lochalsh, Moray Badenoch & Strathspey, Argyll & The Islands, Lochaber, and Inverness & Nairn.

HIE's budget in its first year of operation is

Copper stills in the Glenfiddich whisky distillery

a healthy £73 million, with about £13 million targeted at training and related activities and £4 million at land renewal and reclamation. It has a considerable challenge to meet, but it has the expertise, the will and the finance to do it.

Crystal-ball gazing is a fascinating, if sometimes dangerous pastime, but let us look ahead to the 21st century. What changes and developments can we expect to see in the Highlands and Islands? In a large, sparsely populated area such as this, communications are of vital importance, and developments here are proceeding along two very different lines.

Firstly, roads are steadily improving. Single-track A-roads are fun for the visitor but an irritation for the resident, particularly for commercial purposes, and by the end of the century there should be no major routes left with such stretches.

Electronic communications are also improving apace. The rapid development of computer technology has meant that businesses of many kinds can be run from remote areas. HIDB and British Telecom have made substantial investment in improving such links, and this programme will continue. The concept of the 'telecottage' in which technology is available to a whole community through one outlet is beginning to take root here too, and has very interesting possibilities.

There may well be significant changes in land use and management. With the reduction in EC support, agriculture may become less profitable. There is a growing realisation that sheep are not the ideal conservers of the environment, being too unselective in their cropping, and very interesting experiments are beginning to be tried in mixed enterprises using different kinds of livestock and woodland on the same area.

There have been proposals for the reintroduction of the musk ox, a benign herbivore that is well suited to the Highlands climate, lives in woodland, and can provide a valuable fibre crop. Many people are urging that a partial reafforestation of the Highlands should begin – not with the alien conifers used for commercial timber production in recent years, but with indigenous trees such as oak and Scots pine, which can provide a crop but also enhance the environment on a sustainable basis.

That word 'sustainable' is likely to come up with increasing frequency. It may replace 'conservation', which has earnt itself an unfortunate reputation for insensitivity, as an acceptable term to cover the wise management of a finite resource. Very many people will be earnestly hoping that two new agencies – HIE and Scottish Natural Heritage, which replaced the former Nature Conservancy Council for Scotland and the Countryside Commission for Scotland in April 1992 – will genuinely work together, instead of standing on opposite sides of an invisible fence, as their predecessors too often seemed to do.

Battles need to be replaced by partnerships, for the good of the priceless landscape and wildlife, and above all for the good of the people: if this can be achieved, there will undoubtedly be many more wings spread in the Highlands and Islands in the years ahead.

An old language renewed

Finally, one area where HIE will continue to offer the support its predecessor upheld so strongly is in the teaching, culture and promotion of the Gaelic language. The old tongue of the Highlands is making a new comeback, with dozens of Gaelic playgroups and adult learning classes now up and running, and a substantial increase in the funding for Gaelic language radio and TV programmes.

The annual Gaelic festival, the National Mod, reaches its centenary in Oban in October 1992, and Gaelic too can look forward with confidence to a future in which it will spread its wings. The HIE brochure says there is 'No Grander Scale, No Fairer Land' than the area it covers; few would disagree with those sentiments.

Hutton oil-drilling platform in Cromerty Firth

Gazetteer

▲ Corrieshalloch Gorge

Each entry in this Gazetteer has the atlas
page number on which the place can be
found and its National Grid reference
included under the heading. An
explanation of how to use the National
Grid is given on page 80.

spin and grind grain, and the Satrosphere, a unique 'hands-on' technology centre.

Old Aberdeen has an atmosphere all its own. Within easy strolling distance of King's College, where the chapel with its fine array of medieval woodcarvings is regularly open to the public, are the restored 18th-century houses of Wrights' and Coopers' Place; the Chanonry where the university professors live in elegant, tree-shaded Georgian mansions; and St Machar's Cathedral, completed early in the 16th century, with its collection of historic charters and a splendid heraldic ceiling.

ABERFELDY

MAP REF: 92NN8549

Low-set beside the sparkling waters of the Tay, Aberfeldy is best approached by the A826, the high road from the south through Glen Cochill. As the road sweeps down towards the town, the mansion houses in wooded grounds along the river valley, the farms and the open moorland summits above them, are

ABERDEEN

MAP REF: 89NJ9305

Although it is the 'capital' of the North Sea oil industry, Aberdeen has many things on its municipal mind besides drilling rigs, multi-national contracts and helicopter flights to production platforms far beyond the grey horizon.

Roses, for instance – in their tens and hundreds of thousands. Aberdeen is a commercial rose-growing centre, and the 100,000 it has planted on the verges and central reservation of its main suburban bypass road help it to be a regular winner in the Britain in Bloom competition.

Appropriately enough, one of the most popular series produced by BBC Television in Scotland is *The Beechgrove Garden*, set in the grounds of the studio in Aberdeen's Beechgrove Terrace.

The city is lavishly supplied with public parks. Duthie Park continues the roses theme, with an entire hillside devoted to them on its site above the River Dee. Seaton Park slopes down to Aberdeen's other river, the Don. Between the two river mouths, two miles of beach have more parkland behind.

On the western outskirts, Hazelhead Park has woodland

nature trails, animal and bird collections, playing fields and three of the many fine golf courses with which the city is surrounded.

In the centre of Aberdeen, Provost Skene's House and Provost Ross's House are beautifully restored 16th-century mansions; the latter houses the city's maritime museum. Marischal College, part of Aberdeen University, has a remarkable granite frontage – a riotous framework of intricate, ornamented pinnacles.

Children will enjoy visiting Jonah's Journey, where they can dress up,

all seen with an impressive mountain skyline beyond.

General Wade's elegant five-arched bridge over the Tay at Aberfeldy was built in 1733. Beside it stands the monument to the Black Watch regiment, erected in the town a few years later.

Off the A826 is the Birks of Aberfeldy nature trail, in the wild ravine of the Falls of Moness. 'Birks' are birches, but the trees in this mile-long glen also include beech and sycamore, oak, ash, hazel, alder and rowan. A quiet approach often

▲ Watermill and mill lade, Aberfeldy

allows visitors to see roe deer browsing. Dippers and wagtails feed in the pools and by the water's edge. Finches, warblers and wood pigeons flit among the varied woodland cover. Castle Menzies, 1 mile west of Aberfeldy on the B846, is a fine example of a 16th-century Z-plan fortified tower house.

ANGUS GLENS
MAP REF: 93NO3954

The long glens that sweep south-eastwards from the high hills of the Eastern Grampians to the fertile lands of Strathmore are famed for their beauty. Each has its own character, and all are worth visiting.

The most southerly is Glen Isla, with at its head the dramatic cliffs of the Caenlochan National Nature Reserve. Forter Castle, recently restored, is a late 16th-century L-plan tower house dominating the glen. The forests above Kirkton of Glenisla are used for cross-country skiing in winter, whilst lower down the glen, Loch of Lintrathen is a Scottish Wildlife Trust reserve noted for its winter wildfowl.

Glen Prosen is the quietest and arguably the most lovely of the glens, with wooded hills rising above its fertile farmland. From the road-end at Kilbo, a noted hill path, the Shank of Drumwhallo, leads over to Glen Clova. On Tulloch Hill is the impressive Airlie Memorial Tower, erected to honour the memory of a former Earl of Airlie killed on active service, and at the roadside is a plaque to the Antarctic explorers Captain Scott and Dr Wilson, who spent some time here planning their expedition.

Glen Clova runs a long 15 miles to Milton of Clova, from where a dead-end road continues a further 4 miles to Glendoll and its youth hostel, a former shooting lodge. From here famous old passes cross the hills to Deeside and Braemar. Shorter walks are laid out in the woods around the hostel. The Clova Inn, at Milton, has long offered hospitality. Nearby is a picnic area with toilets, and a right of way leads behind the hotel, uphill to Loch Brandy, gloriously set in a hanging corrie below cliffs.

The three glens of Isla, Proven and Clova meet at the market town of Kirriemuir, where the National Trust for Scotland has restored the birthplace of J M Barrie, author of *Peter Pan*.

The most northerly of the Angus Glens is Glenesk. From its head, 17 miles north of Kirriemuir, another very old route leads past the Queen's Well, at which Queen Victoria is said to have taken refreshment, and over Mount Keen, the most easterly 3,000ft mountain in Scotland, to Deeside. This too is a long glen; lower down, past Tarfside is The Retreat, a museum of local life, and the River North Esk can be followed to Edzell, where the castle has a famous formal garden.

APPLECROSS
MAP REF: 86NG7144

The Pass of the Cattle to Applecross is one of the most stunning roads in Britain. After a steep but steady ascent, hairpin bends fling it to a summit at 2,053ft, with an eagle's-eye view of the towering cliffs back towards Loch Kishorn.

Easier gradients take the road down across a deserted moorland with dozens of silvery hill lochs, before dipping towards the forested valley and sweeping sand bay of Applecross village itself.

South of the village is a coastline of sheltered inlets and rocky points, fishing and crofting hamlets. To the north, a through-road opened in the 1970s heads for the tip of Applecross peninsula. The seaward views are magnificent, across the Inner Sound to the mountain peaks of Skye, often silhouetted against the fiery splendours of a West Highland sunset.

▼ The hills of Skye at sunset from the summit of the Pass of the Cattle in Applecross

ARDNAMURCHAN

MAP REF: 90NM4167

This is the most westerly parish on the British mainland. From the lighthouse on Ardnamurchan Point there is a breathtaking view of open sea and islands: Coll and Tiree; the Small Isles of Rum, Eigg and Muck; Skye and, on a clear day, the whole line of the Outer Hebrides.

The main road through Ardnamurchan is the dead-end B8007, which hugs the bays of the southern coast on its way to Kilchoan, the main village of the district. The 18th-century parish church is there, and nearby are the ruins of Mingary Castle, now an Ancient Monument but once the stronghold of the MacIans of Ardnamurchan.

Minor roads meander across the peninsula to the crofting and fishing settlements on the north coast. There are fine sandy beaches at Sanna, Portuairk, Plocaig, Achateny and Kilmory.

Much of Ardnamurchan is red deer country. Golden eagles and peregrine falcons nest, while sea-birds feed in the multitude of bays, and seals have their favourite rocks for reclining in the sun.

The remote Ardnamurchan lighthouse, the most westerly point on the mainland of Britain ▼

BALLATER

MAP REF: 89NO3696

Royal Deeside's principal town is neatly planned, with granite houses and hotels laid out in a grid pattern of streets dating from the late 18th century, when it was developed as a spa resort for visitors who came to sample the waters of Pannanich Wells, just east of the settlement. On the other side of the town is the steep-sided Craigendarroch – crag of oaks, where well-maintained paths run through the woods to the summit viewpoint; part of the lower hill has been developed as a leisure and timeshare resort.

Other walks cross the bridge over the Dee and continue up the steeply wooded slopes of Craig Coillich – crag of the cockerel – and along the Old Line, a projected extension of the railway towards Braemar, which starts at the golf course and follows a ledge above the Dee towards Bridge of Gairn. The railway – once regularly used by the Royal Family – closed in 1966, and 4 miles of the trackbed to Cambus o'May are now open as a footpath and bridleway.

South-west of Ballater, a minor road runs down Glen Muick past Birkhall, owned by the Queen Mother, to Loch Muick below famous Lochnagar, celebrated in verse by Byron and more recently in a children's story, *The Old Man of Lochnagar*, written by the Prince of Wales. This whole area is a nature reserve run by the Scottish Wildlife Trust and Balmoral Estate. There is a visitor centre at Spittal of Glenmuick, and walks lead round the loch and up into the hills.

BANCHORY

MAP REF: 89NO6995

At Scottish country dances all over the world, much of the foot-tapping music for jigs, reels and strathspeys was written by a Banchory man. A memorial in the High Street of this attractive Deeside town recalls Scott Skinner, the famous fiddler/composer who was born here in 1843.

▲ Fed by hill burns, the rushing Water of Feugh foams under the Bridge of Feugh in Banchory

Banchory is an invigorating, open-air holiday resort. There are walks in the woodlands north-west of the town; along the banks of the Dee on the edge of the well laid-out golf course; to the salmon leap at the Bridge of Feugh; and south-west of the town through birchwoods and conifer plantations to the viewpoint summit of Scolty Hill.

Permits for salmon and sea-trout fishing on the Dee are available in Banchory, and there are facilities for tennis, bowling, football and cricket. Banchory is an ideal centre for visiting the Castles of Mar (see page 35).

BANFF

MAP REF: 89NJ6863

This former county town is a showpiece of 18th-century architecture, although its history goes back to the 12th century, when it was a prosperous member of the Hanseatic trading league.

Beside the River Deveron there is a parkland golf course called Duff House Royal. It takes its name from William Adam's baroque Georgian

mansion built for the 1st Earl of
Fife. Duff House is unfurnished, but
the fabric is maintained and it is
open to the public. Banff Museum
has interesting displays of arms and
armour and mementos of the life of
the 18th-century astronomer, James
Ferguson, a Banffshire man.

Up-river, a woodland walk leads to
the high-level Bridge of Alvah, built
in 1772, where the Deveron spins
through a rock-walled gorge.

Anglers fish the Deveron for trout
and salmon, but commercial fishing-
boats have mostly moved away, and
Banff harbour is largely recreational.

In summer, a narrow-gauge railway,
sometimes with steam-hauled trains,
runs regular services from a station
near the harbour to the beach at
Banff Links.

BENNACHIE
MAP REF: 89NJ6522

A prominent landmark, Bennachie is
one of the great hill-walking ranges
of north-east Scotland. From the
Donview Visitor Centre on the south
side of the range, as well as from car
parks to the east and north, a
network of forest roads and
footpaths climbs through
plantations of spruce, pine and larch
on to breezy heather moorlands. It
finally peaks at the summits of
Craigshannoch, Oxen Craig – at
1,733ft the highest point – and the
Mither Tap, one of the most striking
hilltops in Scotland, defended on
one side by shattered granite cliffs.

These are splendid viewpoints. In
really clear weather the northerly
outlook extends as far as the hills of
Caithness, more than 70 miles away.

Roe deer and squirrels live in the
plantations. An ancient track called
the Maiden's Causeway can be traced
on the north-east shoulder of the
range. Bennachie is held in great
affection by Aberdeenshire folk and
the hill has its own conservation
group, the Bailies of Bennachie.

The Mither Tap, highest point of Bennachie
in Aberdeenshire ▼

BLACK ISLE
MAP REF: 88NH6548

Access to the Black Isle – not an
island but a long peninsula – has
been made very much easier by the
construction of the Kessock Bridge
leading from Inverness and the
bridge over the Cromarty Firth. At
North Kessock, the tourist
information centre has plenty of
literature on the area.

The Black Isle is ideal for quiet
sightseeing and walking, with many
excellent coastal walks at Fortrose,
Rosemarkie, Cromarty and
elsewhere. Fortrose has its 14th-
century cathedral and at Rosemarkie
you should not miss Groam House
Museum with its fine collection of
Pictish artefacts including a splendid
inscribed stone.

Cromarty's neat harbour is still
used by fishing boats, and in Church
Street is Hugh Miller's Cottage,
restored by the National Trust for
Scotland to mark the life and work
of the pioneer 19th-century
geologist. The town's jail is currently
being adapted as a visitor attraction.

The Black Isle is well wooded and
you can walk to the summit of
Mount Eagle, highest point on the
peninsula, from where the Cromarty
and Moray Firths can be seen – the
former with its flotilla of off-duty
oilrigs usually in evidence. The
Moray Firth is home to one of
Britain's few colonies of dolphins,
which can sometimes be seen off
Chanonry Point.

BLAIR ATHOLL
MAP REF: 88NN8765

This is the village outside the gates
of Blair Castle, home of the Duke of
Atholl, chief of the Murrays. His
Atholl Highlanders are the only
legally recognised private army in
Europe, following a privilege granted
by Queen Victoria.

From the A9, the white towers of
the castle rise above wooded
parkland. The oldest part is
Cumming's Tower, built about 1270.
More than thirty rooms are open to
the public, from April to October.
Most notable of them are the
splendid drawing room and dining
room, with the white marble
chimney-pieces and lavishly
ornamented stucco ceilings.

There are walks and nature trails in
the castle grounds. In the village
itself, a working corn mill and a
rural museum are open to visitors
during the summer.

About three miles west of Blair
Atholl is the Clan Donnaohaidh
Museum at Bruar. Open from April
to October, it features the history of

the Robertsons, Reids and Duncans.
Woodland paths and bridges lead to
the nearby Falls of Bruar.

BRAEMAR
MAP REF: 88NO1591

One of the highest villages in
Scotland, Braemar is at the heart of
Upper Deeside. It is an excellent
walking centre. From a car park near
the top of Chapel Brae, footpaths
meander through the lower slopes of
Morrone Nature Reserve, noted for
its birch and juniper woods. The
adventurous can climb to the
2,815ft summit, which commands
extensive views.

More easily attained is Creag
Choinnich to the east of the town,
reached from the car park on
Glenshee Road. The short, steep
scramble up Creag Choinnich
(Kenneth's Crag) is rewarded by a
glorious view back over the village
to the Cairngorm Mountains beyond.

Next to the Glenshee Road car
park, from where you can see the
cottage in which Robert Louis
Stevenson wrote the first draft of
Treasure Island in 1881, are the
ruins of Kindrochit Castle, dating
from the 14th century. More recent
history is marked at the Invercauld
Arms Hotel, which stands on the
point where the Earl of Mar raised
the standard to set off the 1715
Jacobite Rising. Braemar Castle, a
mile east of the village, was a
Jacobite stronghold and then a
Government barracks, before
reverting to the Farquharsons of
Invercauld in the 1830s. It is open
from May to October.

On the first Saturday in September
each year, the village is packed for
the famous Braemar Gathering,
usually attended by the Queen and
other members of the Royal Family.
Spectators watch the full range of
events, including tossing the caber,
highland dancing and piping.
Quieter pursuits can be found on
Braemar's 18-hole golf course beside
the Clunie Water, and on the Dee, a
noted salmon river.

The minor road which heads west
from Braemar leads to the Linn
o'Dee, where the river foams and
thrashes through a narrow rocky
channel crossed by a bridge opened
by Queen Victoria in 1857. From
Inverey the Princess Walk passes
through fine woods to the waterfall
at the Linn of Corriemulzie. The
road ends at the Linn of Quoich,
from where the Quoich Water can be
followed past curious rock
formations such as the Earl of Mar's
Punchbowl towards the superb high
tableland of Beinn a'Bhuird and Ben
Avon.

An attractive scene in Fraserburgh Harbour, still an energetic fishing port with many of its old houses and buildings now finely restored ▶

BUCHAN

MAP REF: 89NJ9551

There are two separate aspects of this north-eastern corner of Scotland – the agricultural heartland and the fishing coast.

The open Buchan countryside is dotted with 'planned' 18th- and 19th-century villages like Cuminestown, New Byth, Mintlaw, New Pitsligo – whose restored cottages stand above commercial peat-mosses – and Stuartfield.

Turriff is a substantial red-sandstone town which hosts the biggest agricultural show in the north-east. At Aberchirder there are, unusually for Buchan, some woodland walks; the 'Foggie Show' there takes that name because almost everybody in the district calls the little town Foggieloan.

Although it is almost entirely a working landscape, Buchan has one of the finest country parks in Scotland, occupying the woodlands and riversides of the Aden estate at Old Deer. The park also houses an Agricultural Heritage Centre with an award-winning exhibition of farming life. Not far away, the ruined Abbey of Deer is a graceful, ancient monument in lawns set above the winding South Ugie Water.

Fyvie Castle, superbly restored by the National Trust for Scotland, has a fine wheel staircase, exceptional paintings, and extensive gardens with a loch.

Buchan fishermen's multi-million pound investment in deep-sea fishing boats and the most up-to-date equipment has made Peterhead the biggest white-fish port in Western Europe.

The other main port is Fraserburgh, which boasts a two-mile beach and, like Peterhead, has an old fishertown of restored houses bypassed by the modern bustle.

Buchan also has many attractively-placed fishing villages of an older, far less industrialised, style.

Gardenstown, Crovie and Pennan are the most spectacularly located, at the foot of seabird cliffs topped by exhilarating headland walks.

THE CAIRNGORMS

MAP REF: 88NH0104

The vast expanse of the Cairngorm Mountains holds within it some of the most majestic landscapes to be found anywhere in Britain. Much of the area is a National Nature Reserve, and its interior can only be penetrated by a long walk-in. There is much to see around the periphery, however, and the building of the road to service the ski centre has greatly increased accessibility to the northern side of the range.

The road ends at over 2,000ft in Coire Cas, with a spur leading into Coire na Ciste. From Coire Cas, footpaths lead across the magnificent Northern Corries and up to the summit of Cairn Gorm itself. On most days, a chairlift operates to the Ptarmigan Restaurant at 3,600ft. The summit of Cairn Gorm holds a weather station giving automatic hourly readings and the highest wind speeds in Britain, well over 100mph, have been recorded here.

In the winter months – and often well into the spring – the pistes are full of skiers. Cairngorm was the first ski centre in Scotland to be fully developed and its extra altitude means it retains snow later into the season. However, the weather cannot be controlled, of course, and during some winters snow is in short supply.

Lower down, from Glenmore Lodge outdoor centre, a short walk leads to the Pass of Ryvoan and the lovely Lochan Uaine (green lochan), said to be inhabited by fairies. One of the famous Cairngorm passes, the Lairig an Laoigh (pass of the calves) starts

Looking south-east from the summit of Cairn Gorm. On the right are the slopes of Ben Macdui, Britain's second highest mountain ▼

from here, swinging over the shoulder of Bynack More to cross the River Avon and continue down Glen Derry to Deeside. The other pass, the Lairig Ghru, climbs through Rothiemurchus Forest to reach a height of 2,700ft before dropping down past the Pools of Dee to follow that river to Braemar.

There have been fierce battles in recent years over the conservation and management of the Cairngorms. These magnificent mountains have a supreme quality of wildness which needs to be nurtured, and for those able to reach their heart, the rewards are great. The high ground with its distinctive pinkish granite is home to the ptarmigan, dotterel and other mountain birds, and holds Loch Avon, Loch Etchachan – frozen for much of the year – and many rare arctic/alpine plants.

CALLANDER

MAP REF: 92NN6208

This has been a busy tourist town since the early 19th century, when the works of Sir Walter Scott – set as they were in a real landscape – encouraged people to come and see the Trossachs for themselves. The process continues today, and the centrepiece of the town is now the Rob Roy and Trossachs Visitor Centre, where the latest techniques are used to interpret the history of the area and its principal characters.

Callander was the 'Tannochbrae' of the famous *Dr Finlay's Casebook* TV series, and the house used is on the road leading up from the town to the Bracklinn Falls, a fine short walk which can be extended to take in Callander Crags, giving magnificent views over the town to Ben Ledi. This – the 'hill of God' – was one of those used for Beltane celebrations, in which the coming of spring was traditionally marked by the lighting of a fire on the summit to encourage the gods to be generous in providing crops.

There are riverside walks along the meadows of the Teith and a cycleway/footpath leads from the town northwards beside Loch Lubnaig all the way to Strathyre. Across the loch on the A84 a car park gives access to the tumbling Falls of Leny. Callander has a fine selection of gift shops, many hotels, and caravan parks.

COMRIE

MAP REF: 92NN7722

Lying exactly on the Highland Boundary Fault, this 18th-century 'planned village', where the River Lednock and the Water of Ruchill

▲ The gardens of Crathes Castle on Deeside are a riot of colour in summer. The castle is owned by the National Trust for Scotland

CASTLES OF MAR

While there are many sturdy fortresses in the old province of Mar, between the upper valleys of the Dee and the Don, the castles in the care of the National Trust for Scotland were intended less as strongholds and more as grandly-designed and opulently-furnished private homes.

Craigievar Castle, in the hills south of Alford, was completed in 1626 by the Bell family of architects and masons for William Forbes, a spectacularly successful Aberdeen merchant in the Baltic trade who was known as 'Danzig Willie'.

This is the classic fairytale castle, whose plain lower floors gradually blossom out into elegantly rounded upper towers and turrets and a rooftop viewing balcony. It is notable for its moulded plaster ceilings, oak panelling and elegant hall complete with musician's gallery.

The Bells were also involved in the building of Crathes Castle near Banchory, although the Burnett lairds had been landowners here for more than two and a half centuries before it was completed in 1596.

Crathes is famous for its original painted ceilings and friezes. Outside, there are eight linked gardens deliberately varied in style and colours, with massive yew hedges planted in 1702.

Farther afield in the 595-acre estate, nature trails wander through varied woodland and open farming country, past ponds and meandering burns.

A little east of Crathes is Drum Castle, a 17th-century mansion linked to an older tower built for the armour-bearer to Robert Bruce, William de Irwin.

Farther north is Castle Fraser, dating from the 1570s and the largest and grandest of the Mar Castles.

meet the River Earn, was once so prone to earth tremors that an Earthquake House was built. It is still standing, and contains illustrations of some of the Victorian earthquake-recording devices. Pegs falling over on the flat earth floor showed the strength and direction of each shock. Although the worst of the tremors were over 100 years ago, many people in the village have tales of dishes suddenly rattling in their cupboards.

Comrie is the home of the Museum of Scottish Tartans, which has displays on individual patterns, the history of Highland dress and a sample of the tartan which reached the moon.

'Comrie Fortnight' every summer features parades, music, guided walks and sporting events. On 31 December, the Old Year is seen out with a torchlight procession.

The Circular Walk in Glen Lednock passes two fine waterfalls on its way through natural woodland, open farmland and forestry plantations. A steep path off the Glen Lednock road leads to the finest viewpoint in the district, the Melville Monument on the summit of Dunmore.

▲ The Armillary Sundial at the Younger Botanic Gardens, Dunoon

Surrounded and deeply indented by sea-lochs, with forested hillsides and magnificent walks, sailing centres and haunts of anglers, famous gardens and an abiding sense of history, Cowal is a Highlands in miniature.

The most direct way into Cowal is by car ferry across the Firth of Clyde to Dunoon or Hunter's Quay. But the most scenic approach is by the A83 from Arrochar. It runs through the mountainous northern fringes of the 100 square-mile Argyll Forest Park, over the Rest and be Thankful, an 860ft pass where the line of the old military road of 1750 is used today for motorsport events. Then it sweeps down through Glen Kinglas to the junction where the A815 turns left into the heart of Cowal.

Soon, the B839 comes in from the east, through the forbiddingly named Hell's Glen, with its claustrophobic hillsides. Over that way, and also reached by the B828 Glen Mhor road which turns off just after the summit of Rest and be Thankful, is Lochgoilhead.

This holiday village at the head of the fjord-like Loch Goil is a centre for hill-walking, pony-trekking, sea-angling, sailing, and water-skiing.

At Strachur the A815 turns inland, to its most impressive, winding stretch along the eastern shore of Loch Eck, a favourite watersports area.

Beyond Loch Eck is the Younger Botanic Garden, open from April to October. The finest feature of the garden's 120 acres is the brilliant display of more than 250 species of rhododendrons, at their most colourful in the late spring and early summer.

Heading in the direction of Dunoon, the A815 comes to Sandbank, where several America's Cup yachts were built. A coast road goes past Lazaretto Point, once the site of a quarantine station, by Hunter's Quay and Kirn. The shorter inland road reaches Dunoon direct by Loch Loskin.

Dunoon has been a holiday resort since Victorian times. There are bowling greens and an 18-hole golf course with wide-ranging views over the Firth of Clyde, walks and trout-stocked reservoirs, sailing and sea-angling. The Cowal Highland Gathering, held every August at Dunoon, is a hectic weekend of piping competitions, Highland dancing and athletics.

Loch Striven is a favourite destination for sailors, but the motorist's way to the head of the loch is back through Dunoon and Sandbank, then off the A815 on to the B836, a narrower and winding road across a much wilder landscape.

▲ Colourful reflections on the surface of a Cowal loch

Clachaig, the only village along it, has a scattered look: the Clyde Gunpowder Mills were built here in Napoleonic times, and it was advisable to keep the buildings well apart.

On the far side of the peninsula between Loch Striven and Loch Riddon, the B836 meets the A886. The left turn here follows the winding shore of Loch Riddon to the strung-out village of Colintraive, from which a car ferry sails to Rhubodach at the north end of the Island of Bute.

Travelling back from Colintraive, past the end of the B836, leads to a road junction at the foot of Glendaruel. The A886 continues up the glen, alongside the trout and salmon waters of the River Ruel, on the shortest way back to Strachur.

But the turn to the south, on to the A8003, leads to some of the most spectacular viewpoints in Scotland, as it climbs high above the coastline then dips down again to Tighnabruaich on the western arm

of the Kyles of Bute, the narrow strait which separates the Island of Bute from the mainland.

Tighnabruaich – Gaelic for 'the house on the bank' – grew up in Victorian times when a steamer pier was built to tap the Clyde coast holiday traffic. Today it is the yachting centre of the Kyles of Bute.

Millhouse used to be the site of another gunpowder factory, supplied with water from two reservoirs to the north. Still known as the Powder Dams, they are stocked with trout and link up with one of the tougher hill-walking routes.

North of Millhouse, the B8000 runs inland through Kilfinan to

An attractive summerhouse in the Younger Botanic Gardens ▼

Otter Ferry, back on Loch Fyne. There was once a ferry here, but 'Otter' is a corruption of the Gaelic *oitir* – a sandy spit which can be seen stretching well out into the loch at low tide.

Last of the little villages of Cowal, as this circular tour links up again with the A886 near Strachur, is Newton. Tucked away on the shore of Loch Fyne, Newton offers many of the traditional attractions of Cowal – peace and quiet, and views over a beautiful loch to the wooded hills.

CRIEFF

MAP REF: 92NN8621

The location of this old-established market town, where the Highlands sweep up from the gentle plain of Strathearn, not only made it a famous cattle-trading centre in the 18th century, but also brought it many misadventures during the Jacobite Risings.

Crieff is on a steeply sloping site above the River Earn. At the highest level, Strathearn Hydro is a Victorian hotel in extensive grounds, established to take advantage of the pure waters of the Turret Burn. These are also supplied to the Glenturret distillery, which dates from 1775.

There are visitor tours of the distillery, as well as of Crieff's more recently founded pottery, paperweight, glass and crystal factories.

Above the Hydro, pathways lead on to the woods and heathland of the Knock. There is a nature trail at Culcrieff on the west side. Crieff golf club covers undulating land towards the east.

About 4 miles south-east of Crieff, along the B8062, is the 17th-century Innerpeffray library, which is still open every day except Thursdays, and has a notable collection of bibles.

CRUDEN BAY

MAP REF: 89NK0936

More than a mile of excellent curving beach here is backed by grassy dunes which themselves give way to a pair of naturally-landscaped golf courses. From 1899 the luxury Cruden Bay Hotel was a top people's social and sporting resort, but it was dismantled after the second world war.

North of the sands, reached by a road past the restored cottages of Port Erroll, the little Water of Cruden – diverted in 1798 – runs into a once-busy fishing harbour. Nets are still dried on the traditional poles, but the fishing is much reduced and the harbour is also used by weekend sailors.

The original course of the river reaches the sea below the cliffs where the ruins of Slains Castle stand ragged against the sky. They are said to have given author Bram Stoker, a regular holidaymaker at Cruden Bay, the inspiration for Count Dracula's castle.

TARTAN

There is a charming legend that tartan was first mentioned in the Old Testament when Joseph wore his coat of many colours. Regrettably it isn't true because the word tartan comes from the French word *tartaine*, a particular kind of French cloth which has nothing to do with colour at all. If Joseph had spoken Gaelic then he would call his Technicolor dream coat *breacan*, which is the Gaelic for a multi-coloured cloth.

The idea does go back a long way. Virgil, half a century before Christ, made reference to 'striped and shiny coats' which is much nearer to the striped linen shirt that the invading Irish introduced to Scotland in the 7th century. It is from these striped shirts that *breacan* (or tartan as we now know it) has descended and, over the years, it became criss-crossed with coloured threads to give a recognisable tartan by the end of the 16th century.

In those days, tartans tended to identify the territorial area in which a man lived, and since families of the same name tended to congregate in the same straths and glens, the particular area tartan became associated with that particular family or clan name.

Today there are several hundred tartans, many of them still attached to a particular clan. A more recent development is for particular concerns (such as Rangers Football Club) to develop and merchandise their own tartans. Legally there is nothing to stop anyone wearing anyone else's tartan although it is highly unlikely that, after years of bitter strife, a Macdonald would be seen alive in a Campbell tartan even if he might be happy to marry a Campbell wife. What is zealously guarded is the word 'tartan'; in courtesy at least, a new tartan (as opposed to a check) has to be approved by the Scottish Lyon King at Arms and by the Standing Council of Scottish Chiefs. But so far nobody has been sent to the Tower (or even to the dungeons of Edinburgh Castle) for flaunting what is, after all, a charming and romantic tradition. With so many official tartans to choose from the chances are that, with a little research, everyone can find one to which he or she can lay even tenuous kinship claim!

Tartans come in every possible shade and pattern of check ▼

▲ The memorial to the Scottish novelist Neil Miller Gunn (1891–1973) looks out over the Ross-shire countryside from its site near Dingwall

DINGWALL
MAP REF: 87NH5458

The administrative centre of the large district of Ross and Cromarty takes its name from the Norse for 'a place of parliament'. It was the birthplace, in around AD1005, of Macbeth, ruler of Scotland from 1040 to 1057.

One of Macbeth's successors, Alexander II, made Dingwall a royal burgh in 1226, and part of its long history is told in the Town House Museum (open May to September) which also features the story of the distinguished soldier Sir Hector MacDonald, who is commemorated by the impressive monument on Mitchell Hill.

DORNOCH
MAP REF: 85NH7989

This graceful little town beside the Dornoch Firth was once a cathedral city. A Bishop of Caithness had the cathedral built in the 13th century. Although it was sacked by the Reformers in 1570, it was later rebuilt and is now the parish church.

More grimly, a memorial stone in a town garden marks the place where Janet Horn, the last woman to be executed in Scotland for witchcraft, was burned at the stake in 1722.

In the former Town Jail is a fine craft centre, where you can see tartan weaving taking place.

Around Dornoch there are miles of safe, sandy beaches. And the splendidly kept Old Course of Royal Dornoch Golf Club offers, in the opinion of many experts, the most northerly first-class golf in the world.

DUFFTOWN
MAP REF: 88NJ3240

In 1817 James Duff, the 4th Earl of Fife, began to lease building plots in the town that took his name. Only six years later, Mortlach Distillery opened on the banks of the Dullan Water.

Now there are seven malt whisky distilleries in the town. One of the main attractions is the supply of peaty water, from the Dullan and the Fiddich, Jock's Well and the Priest's Well. Visitors are given guided tours, on weekdays, of Glenfiddich Distillery, which is also the start of a motoring Malt Whisky Trail (see page 55). Next to the distillery are the ruins of Balvenie Castle, a 13th-century Comyn stronghold.

Pleasant walks around Dufftown include one to Mortlach church, on a site used for worship since 566, then up the wooded banks of the Dullan past the Linen Apron waterfall.

OSPREYS

After being lost as a breeding species since Edwardian times, ospreys – at first only one pair – began to nest again in the Highlands in the 1950s. In the early days of the re-introduction, egg-collectors ruined conservationists' attempts to safeguard the nesting sites. They are still a serious problem, but happily the birds are now well established. Up to 30 pairs nest in the Highlands every season, in two publicised locations and many more which are closely guarded secrets.

▲ The return of the osprey has been one of the great success stories of conservation in Scotland in recent years

The ospreys winter in West Africa and arrive in Scotland in April. Different pairs return to the RSPB reserve in the pine woods near Loch Garten, between Aviemore and Nethy Bridge, and to the Scottish Wildlife Trust reserve at Loch of the Lowes, north-east of Dunkeld. Visitors are welcome at these sites, where close observation of the nests is possible. Other wildlife displays are mounted at both reserves.

Eggs hatch in June, and the ospreys have usually headed back towards Africa by the end of August. During the four months in between, these substantial birds of prey may be seen hunting for food in lochs near the nesting sites, swooping dramatically for fish which they snatch up in their powerful talons.

◄ Gleaming copper stills at the Glenfiddich Distillery in Dufftown: visitors are welcome throughout the year

DUNKELD

MAP REF: 92NO0242

Steeply wooded crags overlooking a double bend on the Tay give Dunkeld a dramatic riverside setting. Above the river stands the ruined medieval cathedral, sacked by the Reformers in 1560 but partly restored. The 13th-century choir is now the parish church.

In 1689 most of Dunkeld was burned to the ground in the aftermath of the Battle of Killiecrankie. Many of the replacement town-centre houses of that period have been beautifully restored. A National Trust for Scotland information centre describes the work involved.

Linked to Dunkeld by a Telford bridge of 1809 is the Victorian village of Birnam. Beatrix Potter's tales of Peter Rabbit and Mr Jeremy Fisher the Frog were written on successive days while she was on holiday at the house called Eastwood, across the Tay from Birnam's riverbank Terrace Walk.

The Tay near here is a famous salmon river, and Dunkeld is an excellent centre for walking. From the A9, just west of the town, a woodland trail goes to the

▲ Looking west over the Kyle of Durness from Keoldale

Hermitage, a summer-house of 1758 beside the Falls of the Braan. There are several Forestry Commission walks around the village of Inver, on the high ground of Craigvinean Forest.

DURNESS

MAP REF: 84NC4067

Standing back from a rugged coast where cliff-faces dip down to sandy coves, and sea-bird colonies far outnumber human settlements, Durness is surrounded by well-tended crofting fields. East of the village is Smoo Cave, the most famous feature in this limestone landscape. Visitors can approach by boat, but detailed exploration is for experienced potholers only.

To the north-west is Faraid Head at the tip of the hilly peninsula. The road to it passes Balnakeil, where there is a craft village, a ruined church of 1619 and a fine west-facing beach backed by sheltering dunes.

At Keoldale on the Kyle of Durness a passenger ferry links up with the May-September minibus service over the wild country of the Parph, where eagles nest and gannets fly the offshore air currents to Cape Wrath. The name comes from a Norse word *hvarf*, meaning a turning-point. The lighthouse there, built in 1827 on top of 400ft cliffs, marks the remote north-western corner of mainland Britain.

Many of the 18th-century houses in Dunkeld have been superbly well restored by the National Trust for Scotland ▼

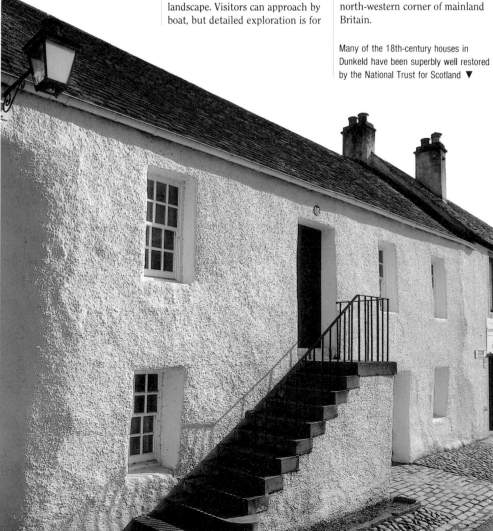

ELGIN

MAP REF: 88NJ2162

As the old county town of Moray, Elgin retains many graceful buildings. Most famous of them is the ruined 13th-century cathedral known as the Lanthorn (Lantern) of the North. It is regarded as the finest of all Scottish cathedrals in design.

Elgin Museum has a famous collection of fossils, and at the west end of the town is an old meal mill with a visitor centre and craft shop.

About 4 miles south-west of the town, the picnic site at Torrieston is the starting point of a network of trails in the hills of Monaughty Forest. In the valley beyond stands Pluscarden Abbey, rebuilt by the community of Benedictine monks who moved there in 1948, after the site had been out of their Order's hands since the Reformation. Visitors are welcome.

North-west of Elgin, the ruins of the 13th-century Duffus Castle, to a Norman motte-and-bailey design, are open to view. A mile farther north is Gordonstoun School, of which several members of the Royal Family are old boys.

On the coast, the five miles of sandy beaches on Burghead Bay can be reached either from the fishing village of Burghead itself, or from the Forestry Commission's picnic site among the pine woods of Roseisle on the B9089.

Elgin Cathedral, known as 'the Lanthorn of the North' ▼

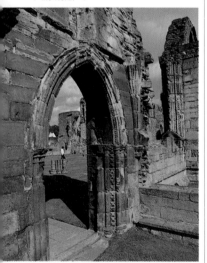

SALMON RIVERS

The best salmon rivers in the Highlands can be fished in a remarkable variety of locations. Some anglers favour the river-banks within the town boundaries of Perth and Inverness. Others wade chest-deep at Grantown in the darkening waters of a Strathspey dusk. There are famous salmon beats in the remote headwaters of northern rivers such as the Oykel and the Halladale; along the wooded banks of the Findhorn and the Deveron; on the Dee and the Don before they meet the North Sea at Aberdeen.

Pride of place among the salmon rivers goes to the Tay. Together with its many tributaries, like the Tummel and the Lyon, it has the greatest catchment area of any river in Britain. More than 10,000 salmon are caught in these waters every season – and that is without counting those netted at commercial stations on the Firth, though this industry has declined greatly in recent years.

The Tay still holds the record for the heaviest salmon ever caught on a British river. Husky anglers have been trying for over 70 years to match the $67\frac{1}{2}$ lb fish taken on the Glendelvine beat downriver from Birnam – after a four-hour struggle – by a no doubt tired, but triumphant, 22-year-old girl, Georgina Ballantine.

The Tay, one of Scotland's finest salmon rivers ▼

FORT WILLIAM

MAP REF: 91NN1074

Situated on the shores of Loch Linnhe, at the southern end of the Great Glen which strikes directly through Scotland from Inverness, Fort William is the trading and transport centre of Lochaber, spreading up the foothills of Ben Nevis, the highest mountain in Britain.

A Government fortress of 1655 was rebuilt much more strongly during the reign of William III and gave the town its name. But the fort was swept away in 1864 to make room for the railway, whose arrival sparked off the building of the modern town. Fort William is one of the principal stations on the West Highland Line from Glasgow. Trains continue beyond it through rugged scenery by Glenfinnan and a famous viaduct, Lochailort, Arisaig and Morar to the herring port of Mallaig and a car-ferry to Skye.

Fort William's West Highland museum includes many relics of Jacobite times, notably the 'secret portrait' of Bonnie Prince Charlie. A wooden board has an apparently random design of daubs of paint. But when a metal cylinder is placed on it, the multi-coloured streaks reflect on its curved surface as a miniature portrait of the Prince.

There are two famous sporting events in Fort William, both testing competitors' stamina to its limits. In May, the town is the base for the Scottish Six Days' Trial, an endurance motor-cycling event which attracts top riders from all over the world. September is the time of the Ben Nevis Race, when runners tackle a course from the Claggan Park to the summit of the 4,406ft-high mountain and back again.

Ben Nevis shows its least spectacular side to the town. From Achintee, at the end of the road along the east side of Glen Nevis, the 'tourist path' climbs to the summit. Although the summit is often shrouded in cloud even when the sun is shining in Fort William, the view from the top on a clear day is magnificent. Southwards are the mountain ridges of the Mamores, west is Ardgour. Much farther away, the view extends to the Cairngorms and the island peaks of Jura and Skye.

On the north side of Ben Nevis are the mighty 2,000ft rock faces, towers, gullies and buttresses which attract climbers, summer and winter. On the plateau itself are the ruins of the observatory established in 1883 by the meteorologist Clement Wragge. This did pioneering work in long-range weather forecasting, before being thoughtlessly closed

▲ The unmistakeable shape of Ben Nevis, Britain's highest mountain and a challenge to walkers of all ages

down in 1904.

For people who prefer lower altitudes, the great spectacle in Glen Nevis is the mile-long gorge among the pines and birches below Steall. It is reached by footpath from the car park at the top of the main Glen Nevis road.

Lower down the glen there are walks in the Forestry Commission plantations which form almost the final stretch of the West Highland Way. More forest walks have been laid out at Leanachan on the Spean Bridge road and at Inchree uphill from Corran Ferry, south of Fort William. This car-ferry is the main link to Ardgour and Ardnamurchan. By the lochside, off the A82, there are some very pleasant picnic sites.

A recent attraction is the gondola of Aonach Mor, Scotland's newest ski resort, 4 miles north of Fort William off the A82. A 10-minute ride leads to the mountain restaurant at 2,000ft with spectacular views.

Perhaps the strangest sight in the mountain country around Fort William is in Glen Roy, north-east of Spean Bridge, from a Nature Conservancy car park and viewpoint. On the hillsides to the north are the 'Parallel Roads', stretching for miles in a horseshoe curve round the glen.

They mark the three different shore levels of an ice age loch, progressively lower as the ice which dammed it melted, until finally water and ice both completely drained away. The whole of the upper glen is a nature reserve with an unspoiled range of hill country, and gives a unique insight into Scotland's glacial past.

GAIRLOCH
MAP REF: 86NG8076

Spread along the shore of a west-facing sea-loch, Gairloch is a self-contained holiday resort in beautifully varied coastal, hill and mountain scenery. It has splendid sands, a golf course where even novices are consoled by the views, sea angling in Loch Gairloch, fishing in rivers and inland lochs, and it is the centre for attractive drives in every direction.

Gairloch village and its satellite settlements like Strath and Auchtercairn are built along the A832 and the B8021 which runs along the north shore of Loch Gairloch. The award-winning Gairloch Heritage Museum is open on weekdays from May till September. The harbour, tucked away in a sheltered bay to the south, is the base of Gairloch Boat Club.

The most intriguing stretch of Loch Gairloch is its southern shore, a series of wooded and rocky inlets. It is reached by the B8056, meandering towards Badachro, where boats may be hired and the bay is completely sheltered by the bulk of Eilean Horrisdale.

▲ The popular holiday village of Gairloch in the Western Highlands enjoys superb seaward views

At Redpoint, where the road ends, there are more sandy bays, grassy dunes and a viewpoint looking west towards Skye, south and east towards the shapely peaks of Torridon.

A superb coastal walk leads south from here to Diabaig, passing the remote youth hostel at Craig.

North-west from Gairloch, the B8021 goes past the camping and caravan sites at Big Sand on the way up the coast to Melvaig, where it can be followed to the former lighthouse at Rubha Reidh, now an adventure holiday centre.

▲ A winter view of Glamis Castle, seat of the Earls of Strathmore and childhood home of Queen Elizabeth the Queen Mother

GLAMIS
MAP REF: 93NO3846

The two main visitor attractions in this pleasant little Angus village could hardly be more different in size and style. In the village itself, the National Trust for Scotland maintains the Kirkwynd Cottages – a row of 17th-century almshouses – as the Angus Folk Museum.

The Kirkwynd is also well-known for its Jacquard loom. Most of these elsewhere are simply display pieces, but the Glamis example is used by the only handloom linen weaver working regularly in Scotland at a craft which used to support entire villages.

North of the village, in wooded parkland bounded by the Dean Water, Glamis Castle is the home of the Bowes-Lyon Earls of Strathmore. The present castle is a massive, ornamentally-towered building of the 17th century, with beautifully furnished state rooms open to visitors.

Elizabeth Bowes-Lyon (the Queen Mother) married the Duke of York, who later became George VI; and Princess Margaret was born at Glamis in 1930.

The kitchen, Angus Folk Museum ▼

GLEN AFFRIC
MAP REF: 87NH2020

Although it has one of the most beautiful landscapes in Scotland, with slender lochs in the valley floor, well-wooded hillsides and a river rising among the 3,000ft mountains at its head, Glen Affric has been greatly altered by two separate interests.

In 1946 the North of Scotland and Hydro-Electric Board dammed the River Affric to create the five-mile Loch Benevean. Its power station at Fasnakyle is unobtrusively located and faced with local yellow sandstone. The two waterfalls in the narrow Affric gorge – the Badger Fall and the Dog Fall – remain as they always were.

Both sides of the glen are cloaked in Forestry Commission plantations. A determined effort is being made to help Glen Affric's remnant of the old Caledonian Pine Forest extend and regenerate. Forest walks and picnic places have been laid out beside the Dog Fall and elsewhere in the glen.

GLENELG
MAP REF: 86NG8119

One of the most exhilarating drives in Scotland is over the narrow, hairpinned pass of Mam Ratagan to Glenelg on the Sound of Sleat. A right turn at Glenelg leads past pleasant picnicking areas to the summer-only car ferry to Kylerhea on Skye. The left turn through the main part of the village passes the substantial ruins of the Hanoverian barracks built after 1719 to keep the Jacobite Highlanders in check.

South of Glenelg, up a side-road along the wooded valley of the Glenbeag River, are the brochs of Dun Telve and Dun Troddan, tall beehive-shaped stone houses occupied 2,000 years ago by families of Picts.

The coast road sweeps over the shoulder of the mountains above

GLENCOE

With its mixture of overwhelming mountain scenery and a tragic history, which includes a massacre of clansmen still bitterly remembered today, no easily-reached glen in Scotland is as atmospheric as Glencoe, especially when cloud and mist are wreathed round its towering peaks and ridges. Certainly no trunk road in Britain seems quite as insignificant as the A82 as it threads its way along the foot of the glen.

From the south-east, the A82 reaches Glencoe over Rannoch Moor, then makes a long gradual descent. It passes a side-road to the left towards the chairlift up to the Glencoe skiing grounds, and the loop road on the right to Kingshouse Hotel, originally a staging post on the 18th-century military road to Fort William.

Another side-road on the left down Glen Etive, before the beautifully proportioned peak of Buachaille Etive Mor – the Great Herdsman of Etive – marks the boundary of the National Trust for Scotland's Glencoe estate. More than 14,000 acres in the glen, including the best rock-climbing areas, are in the Trust's hands; access to them is unrestricted.

This is the start of the 'real' Glencoe, and although the mountains themselves are for rock-climbers, several more straightforward walking routes cut through them. Set among a patch of woodland to the right of the main road, the house of Altnafeadh marks the start of the Devil's

Staircase over the northern ridge to Kinlochleven. This hairpinned route was part of the military road. Now it is included in the West Highland Way and – more incongruously – is used every year by motorcyclists competing in the Scottish Six Days' Trial.

Opposite Altnafeadh, a footbridge over the River Coe leads to one of several walking tracks into the steep-sided glens on the south side. All these routes are, of course, for properly-equipped and experienced hill-walkers.

Beyond Loch Achtriochtan in the valley floor, the main road swings right, out of the most precipitous part of Glencoe, to the National Trust for Scotland's visitor centre, open daily from April to October. Here there is a description of the events of the massacre of February 1692, when a party of troops billetted on the MacDonalds of Glencoe rose in the night and, acting on secret orders, tried to murder all their hosts – the clan chief and his wife, men, women and children.

A footpath from the visitor centre, over a bridge across the Coe, leads through woodlands to Signal Rock, where, according to tradition, the signal to start the attack was given. Another walk from the same place goes to a fine viewpoint at An Torr, looking eastwards into the mountainous heart of the glen and north to the great gully above Clachaig Inn. That gully is one of the boundaries of the 'cauldron

subsidence' caused in prehistoric times, when the centre of the volcano which occupied most of modern Glencoe collapsed, and a huge outpouring of molten granite surged up in its place.

The village of Glencoe is on much lower ground, near the shore of Loch Leven. It lies along both sides of the old Glencoe road, superseded by the present one in the 1930s. Halfway towards another bridge over the Coe is the Glencoe and North Lorn Folk Museum, open on weekdays from May to September. Close by is St Mary's church, with its memorial to the last of the MacDonald chiefs of Glencoe, who died in 1894. A side-road to the right, immediately before the bridge, leads to the monument to the MacDonalds killed in 1692.

The village is dominated by the splendidly regular conical peak of Sgor na Ciche, the 2,430ft Pap of Glencoe. Beyond the bridge, a turning to the left leads to the Lochan Trail, laid out by the Forestry Commission in the woodlands on its lower slopes. Centrepiece of the trail is the walk round the lochan itself, with rhododendrons in profusion along the edges and a bordering hillside of tall Corsican pines. One sight no visitor to Glencoe should miss is the reflection of the Pap of Glencoe, and other mountains as the circular walk progresses, mirrored on a calm day in the clear waters of this most attractive ornamental lake.

Loch Hourn. A forest track leads down to Sandaig, the site of 'Camusfearna' in Gavin Maxwell's *Ring of Bright Water.*

Once out of the forest, the road plunges down to Arnisdale and Corran, beautifully situated villages on the north shore of Loch Hourn. Across the loch are the 3,000ft-high peaks of Knoydart. The road ends at Corran, a cluster of houses, where in spring the gardens are a blaze of daffodils.

▲ The magnificent viaduct at Glenfinnan. Steam trains run regular trips on the line in summer

GLENFINNAN
MAP REF: 90NM8980

The A830 road from Fort William to Mallaig has been greatly improved in recent years as far as Lochailort, but the temptation to pass through Glenfinnan without stopping should be resisted. It was here, in August 1745, that Bonnie Prince Charlie raised his standard, setting in train the dramatic events of the next nine months which are known to us today as 'the '45' Jacobite Rising.

The story is very well told in the National Trust for Scotland visitor centre at the roadside (open Easter to October) and a short walk leads to the monument with its superb view down Loch Shiel. The monument was erected by Macdonald of Glenaladale in 1815 and the figure atop it is not the Prince, as is often surmised, but simply a Highlander.

Each August, a gathering is held to mark the start of the Rising, and at the same time of year the Glenfinnan Highland Games take place. The backdrop to all this is the superb viaduct carrying the railway across the glen. Steam trains run along this line in the summer months.

A little west of Glenfinnan is Loch nan Uamh (loch of the cave) where a memorial stone marks the point where the Prince first set foot on the Scottish mainland. It was from here also that he sailed away in autumn 1746, never to return.

The dramatic mountainscape of Glencoe, with Aonach Dubh, one of the famous 'Three Sisters', prominent on the left ▼

GLEN LYON

MAP REF: 91NN5245

From the high-level reservoir of Loch Lyon in the remote mountains of Mamlorn – part of the massive, but generally unobtrusive, Breadalbane hydroelectric scheme – the River Lyon winds down a narrow valley to the comfortable village of Fortingall. Its course of more than 30 miles is through the longest glen in Scotland. An attractive roadway follows the often wooded riverside between towering hills given over mostly to sheep and deer.

Fortingall village owes its thatched houses to a late-Victorian landlord. In the churchyard, the Fortingall yew is one of the oldest living things in Europe, planted at least 1,500 years ago. Even further back into the mists of history, if a local tradition is true, this is where Pontius Pilate was born, while his father guarded the hills and glens with a Roman legion.

GOLSPIE

MAP REF: 85NH8399

A self-contained place, and the administrative centre of Sutherland, Golspie grew up after the early 19th-century clearances on the inland parts of the 1st Duke of Sutherland's estates. But St Andrew's church was built in 1619, although its canopied pulpit and 'laird's loft' are from a century later.

Behind a long sandy beach there is a fine links golf course. On the road to Littleferry and the tidal flats of the Loch Fleet nature reserve, a kart-racing track which attracts competitors from all over Scotland is hidden in the dunes.

There are enjoyable climbing walks in the pine woods behind the town, and along the paths and rustic bridges in Dunrobin Glen. Two miles north of the town is Dunrobin Castle. Seat of the present Duke of Sutherland, it was extended in the 19th century and has gardens modelled on those at Versailles.

The fairytale turrets of Dunrobin, seat of the Dukes of Sutherland ▼

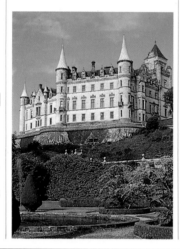

▲ The dramatic outline of Inveraray Castle, seat of the Dukes of Argyll. The castle is open to viewing in the summer months

HUNTLY

MAP REF: 89NJ5339

Once the stronghold of the Gordons – and Gordon is still the district name today – Huntly was extended according to a street plan drawn up by the Duke of Gordon in 1776. Two architecture trails start from Huntly Museum in the town square.

Castle Street leads to an avenue past the Gordon Schools – founded, inevitably, by a Duchess of Gordon in 1839 – to Huntly Castle. The first castle, on a mound above the banks of the River Deveron, was in Norman style. The present ruins are of a much grander castle built at the start of the 17th century by a Marquess of Huntly impressed by the Renaissance architecture of a château on the Loire.

Southwards off the B9002 near Kennethmont is Leith Hall, a 17th-century house and 236-acre hillside estate owned by the National Trust for Scotland. The house is open from May to September; the gardens and nature trails are open all year.

INVERARAY

MAP REF: 91NN0908

In the 1740s, the 3rd Duke of Argyll began the 50-year task of building Inveraray Castle in its wooded parkland above Loch Fyne. Unfortunately, the old burgh of Inveraray stood in the way, so he

HYDROELECTRIC POWER

Although the first privately-operated hydroelectric power stations in Scotland were built in the 1890s, large-scale development of this natural resource was delayed until the establishment, in 1943, of the North of Scotland Hydro-Electric Board. The Board, recently privatised as Scottish Hydro Electric, provides power over a quarter of the total land-mass of Britain.

Many of its later developments harmonise remarkably well with their surroundings. Power stations are often faced with authentic local stone. At Pitlochry, the creation of the winding and wooded Loch Faskally has added one more attraction to an already beautiful scene.

Pitlochry is also the site of the best-known of the Board's fish-passes, built to allow salmon unrestricted access, beyond the dam, to their spawning grounds upstream. Through glass panels, visitors can watch the salmon battling their way against the flow, just as they do in a natural river.

The most spectacular place open to the public in the Board's extensive domain is the power station literally *under* Ben Cruachan, on the A85 20 miles east of Oban. Visitors are taken in a minibus, along an access road through a tunnel two-thirds of a mile long, to the generating hall, 120ft high, in the very heart of the mountain.

◄ The hydroelectric power station on Loch Faskally at Pitlochry, with the famous fish pass on the left

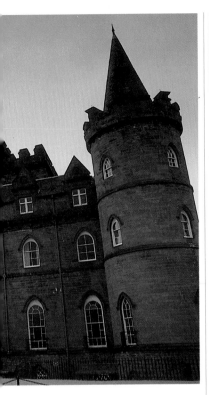

The 16th-century Abertarff House in Inverness is the National Trust for Scotland's Highland headquarters

had it demolished and a new town, in the best spirit of Georgian architecture and planning, established nearby.

A full-scale restoration project that began back in 1957, has seen most of the Georgian public and domestic buildings completely renovated. Their white-washed walls reflect in the waters of a tidal bay.

Inveraray Castle itself – still the home of the Dukes of Argyll, chiefs of Clan Campbell – is open to the public from April to October, although closed on Fridays except in July and August. At Cherry Park in the grounds, a Combined Operations Museum recalls Inveraray's role as a second world war Commando training base.

An excellent walk to a magnificent hilltop viewpoint starts in the castle grounds, while in the town, there is a lower-level viewpoint at a bell-tower built in the 1920s with a famous peal of bells installed as a Campbell war memorial.

South of Inveraray, the Loch Fyneside road passes the Argyll Wildlife Park to reach the farming museum at the old township of Auchindrain, and the spectacular woodland gardens in Crarae Glen.

INVERNESS

MAP REF: 88NH6645

Inverness, the capital of the Highlands, spreads along the banks of the River Ness. Near the Victorian Town House, an excellent local museum and art gallery is open on weekdays throughout the year. On the hilltop above the museum, Inverness Castle is an imposing building of delicate red sandstone, built between 1834 and 1847 as a Sheriff Court and jail. Outside the castle is a statue of Flora Macdonald, who helped Bonnie Prince Charlie escape to Skye in 1746.

There is a pleasant walk along the riverside, over footbridges on to the wooded Ness Islands. A steeper forest trail, west of the town, goes to the summit of Craig Phadrig, possibly the location of the fortress-capital of the Pictish kings.

Culloden Moor, site of the last pitched battle on British soil, which ended the Jacobite Rising in 1746, is 4 miles east of Inverness on the B9006. The National Trust for Scotland visitor centre there is open from March to October.

North-east of Inverness, the mid-18th-century Fort George is on a heavily-defended peninsula into the Moray Firth. Although Fort George is still a military establishment, part of it is open as an Ancient Monument, and it also houses the regimental museums of the Seaforth and the Cameron Highlanders.

INVERURIE

MAP REF: 89NJ7721

Built where the River Urie, meandering desperately over an all but level valley floor, finally manages to merge with the Don, this is a substantial town in its own right, as well as the main shopping and business centre for the district of Garioch – known as 'the Geerie'.

Inverurie is ringed by a great number of prehistoric sites, from 4,000-year-old circles of standing stones to Pictish carvings. Some of these are to be found in the cemetery, which was an important location in later Pictish times: the grassy hill within the cemetery bounds was the site of a long-disappeared Norman castle.

Nearby, across the Don, the suburb of Port Elphinstone justifies its name because it was the start of a 19th-century canal to Aberdeen. There is a display of canal relics in the fine museum in Inverurie's market place.

The River Ness and St Andrew's Cathedral, Inverness ▼

▲ The magnificent Duncansby Stacks, which can be seen by taking a short walk from the lighthouse at Duncansby Head, the true north-eastern corner of mainland Britain. These stunning coastal features are created by the erosion of softer bands of rock

JOHN O' GROATS

MAP REF: 85ND3872

John o' Groats is a white-painted place of pilgrimage and every year quite a few people try to reach it on foot from Land's End. Others do it on roller-skates or pushing prams. Many of them believe that they are travelling from the southernmost point of Britain to the northernmost. Neither is true. Dunnet Head is the most northerly point but it has only a lighthouse to offer, while John o'

Groats has a pleasant village of attractive cottages and a handful of souls, except on summer days when tourists arrive by the coach-load to take a quick glance across the Pentland Firth and a long browse through the souvenir shops.

The more intrepid take advantage of the ferryboat which sails at regular intervals across the spectacular Pentland Firth to South Ronaldsay in Orkney, passing on the way the lonely little island of Stroma inhabited by only sheep and a host of sea-birds. Is the ferryman a descendant of his predecessor of long ago – Jan de Groot, who came to Scotland from Holland and became the ferryman in the village to which he gave his name?

Two miles east of John o' Groats is Duncansby Head, where a short walk leads to a spectacular view of the Duncansby Stacks, three rock pillars in the sea.

KILLIECRANKIE

MAP REF: 92NN9162

A battlefield, a village and a chasm through which the River Garry tumbles between steeply-wooded cliffs all take the same name here – a name derived from the Gaelic for 'wood of aspens'. The Pass of Killiecrankie, now owned by the National Trust for Scotland, was the scene of the first major battle involving Jacobite forces, in summer 1689. The rebels were victorious, but the loss of their leader, 'Bonnie Dundee', led to the collapse of the rebellion.

The NTS visitor centre tells the whole story and also has displays on the landscape and wildlife of the area. There are several walks in the gorge and the adjoining Falls of Tummel area, also owned by the NTS. The woods here are particularly fine in the autumn months, and you can see the Soldier's Leap where a member of the defeated army is said to have hurled himself across in an effort to escape pursuing Jacobites – an awe-inspiring prospect.

KINTAIL

MAP REF: 87NG9319

The Five Sisters of Kintail are among the most shapely mountain peaks in

The Soldier's Leap in the Pass of Killiecrankie, said to have been jumped by an escapee after the battle here in 1689 ▼

▲ The royal deer forests of Balmoral rising to Lochnagar

DEER FORESTS

There are four species of wild deer in the Highlands. Fallow deer and Japanese Sika deer were originally established in deer parks, like the fallow deer on the Loch Lomond island of Inchlonaig. Roe deer are much more widespread, in woodlands and on the hills.

The *Monarch of the Glen*, however, the subject of Sir Edwin Landseer's famous Victorian painting, is undoubtedly the red deer, Scotland's biggest native wild animal. Something like 200,000 live in the Highlands and Islands.

In many areas, red-deer stalking is an important part of the local economy. High rentals are paid for good stalking grounds, and venison is exported. Stalking takes place among the lonely crags and corries of the deer forests – but these are forests almost entirely without trees.

The main stag stalking season is from mid-August to October 20, and during that period hill-walkers and climbers should always check whether they are likely to disturb a carefully-organised stalk.

In summer, red deer are usually high in the hills, feeding on the new season's grass. But they will sometimes be seen late at night, dramatically caught in the beam of a car's headlights, as they cross a road on the way to drink from the river in a glen.

Scotland. As the A87 road comes down to the sea at Loch Duich, through Glen Shiel, the south-western boundary of the range, it passes the site of the battle of 1719. It was here that Spanish troops, supporting the abortive Jacobite Rising, were put to flight.

Like other hill ground in Kintail, the Five Sisters are owned by the National Trust for Scotland, which has an information centre at Morvich, on a bypassed stretch of the old main road.

Loch Duich is forested on both sides. The narrow minor road, from Shiel Bridge below the hill plantations of Ratagan Forest to Totaig, continues as a footpath to an exhilarating viewpoint over sea-lochs and mountains.

Across Loch Duich at Dornie on the A87, a causeway leads to the island fortress of Eilean Donan which was reduced to rubble by a naval bombardment during the 1719 Rising. Completely restored in the 1930s, the castle is open daily from April to October.

KYLE OF LOCHALSH

MAP REF: 86NG7627

Beyond Dornie the A87 enters the district of Lochalsh, much of which is included in the National Trust for Scotland's Balmacara estate. Balmacara village has a picnic site by the shore of Loch Alsh, and a fine variety of hill and woodland walks. Down a side-road there are meandering pathways through the Trust's Lochalsh Woodland Garden, which is open all year. A visitor centre is open from April to October.

After Balmacara, the A87 reaches Kyle of Lochalsh, the car-ferry port for the short crossing to Skye. There are plans for a toll-bridge here, to be built in the mid-1990s.

Kyle is the shopping, trading and transport centre of the district. A short walk to the summit of the Ploc of Kyle shows off the coastline of rugged, rocky bays; reefs and offshore islands; and – across the narrow strait – the hill and mountain country of Skye.

North-east of Kyle, on a winding inlet of Loch Carron, Plockton is one of the most beautifully situated villages in Scotland, with palm-trees growing in lochside gardens and mountains all around. This is an excellent centre for walking and sailing, and has its own popular summer regatta.

◄ The Five Sisters of Kintail, one of the most distinctive mountain outlines in Scotland, soar impressively above the waters of Loch Duich

47

IRON-WORKING

Scotland's earliest ironworks were in the Highlands, where huge tracts of natural woodland were felled to provide charcoal for the furnaces in which imported ore was smelted. As early as 1607 the native oakwoods of Loch Maree were being plundered. Now, only the place-name Furnace on the north-eastern shore remains as an incongruous reminder, among the mountains, of a long-gone trade.

Of the many charcoal ironworks – or 'bloomeries' – in the Highlands, the best known is the Lorn Furnace at Bonawe on the southern shore of Loch Etive, near the village of Taynuilt. Richard Ford and Company of Furness in Lancashire, using ore shipped in from Ulverston, produced its first iron here in 1753.

The Lorn Furnace, by then hopelessly out of date, went out of business in the 1870s. Rescued from dereliction and carefully restored, it is now open as an Ancient Monument. Part of the woodland which provided its charcoal is preserved too, in the twin National Nature Reserve and Forest Nature Reserve in Glen Nant, to the south. The old charcoal-burners' tracks can still be walked on a nature trail, and the coppiced oakwoods show that, here at least, the ironmasters worked with some sense of the need to conserve supplies.

Loch Awe, which stretches south-westward for over 20 miles from Taynuilt to Ford in Argyll, is one of the largest inland lochs in Scotland, and is of supreme beauty throughout ▶

LAIRG

MAP REF: 84NC5806

The most important road centre in the heart of Sutherland, with a station on the Inverness–Wick railway, Lairg has been settled for a very long time. The moorlands all around are dotted with the sites of prehistoric cairns and Stone Age dwellings.

Nowadays, Lairg is best known for its livestock sales and for being a place which provides fine trout and salmon fishing. It is at the southern end of Loch Shin, which has fish-passes at its hydroelectric dam to allow salmon free passage upstream. South of the loch, the River Shin passes through a narrow, wooded valley. There is a famous salmon leap at the Falls of Shin, reached by a Forestry Commission trail.

LOCH AWE

MAP REF: 90NM9710

The north shore of Loch Awe is reached by the A85 Dalmally–Oban road, which squeezes between the lochside and the great bulk of Ben Cruachan at the steep-sided Pass of Brander. On the lochside there, the North of Scotland Hydro-Electric Board's visitor centre is open from April to October and offers a minibus ride to the turbine room deep in the heart of the mountain.

Lochawe village has several hotels which offer trout and salmon fishing. St Conan's Kirk, completed in 1930, includes a deliberate but bewildering variety of architectural styles. Between here and Dalmally is the ruined Campbell stronghold of

Kilchurn Castle, open to view all year.

The east side of Loch Awe is reached by the beautifully wooded A819, and then the winding B840 by Portinnisherrich and the fringe of Eredine Forest to Ford. From there, a narrow road with blind summits heads back up the west side through the plantations of Inverliever and Inverinan. The Forestry Commission has several walks and trails here, with splendid views and varied wildlife.

At Kilchrenan, a dead-end road leads to Ardanaiseig Gardens, with conifers, maples and flowering

HIGHLAND CLEARANCES

Many places in the Highlands have not always been as deserted as they are today. Long-ruined cottages and the encroachment of rushes where once-cultivated land has gone back to the wild are clear evidence of that.

There were several causes of Highland depopulation in the 18th and 19th centuries – too many people for the land; a potato famine; the appeal of making a better life overseas.

But many great landowners and their agents decided to make more money from their estates through renting the land for sheep-farming and, later, for deer-stalking, than

shrubs. The gardens are open from April to October. Back-tracking to Kilchrenan, the last link in the circuit of Loch Awe is the road through Glen Nant and its forest reserves, which rejoins the A85 near Taynuilt.

LOCH EARN

MAP REF: 91NN6223

Lochearnhead is a popular centre for water-skiing, and the loch is also busy with dinghy sailors, canoeists and trout fishermen. The A85 runs past wooded bays and picnic places on the north shore to St Fillans, could be raised from subsistence-level smallholders.

Many of the evictions, notably in Sutherland and in Knoydart, were brutal. Men, women and children, the elderly, the sick and the infirm were thrown out of their homes, which were then demolished. They had no option but to emigrate, move to the cities or to one of the settlements newly established on the coast.

Smallholders had no legal protection until the first Crofters Act of 1886. By then, many of the glens were already deserted. 'Clearances' is all too bland a word for the deliberate policy of emptying a countryside to make way for sheep and deer.

▲ The ruins of Kilchurn Castle, at the north end of Loch Awe, are in the care of Historic Scotland and are open to view

CROFTING

Although many Highland estates cover tens of thousands of acres, something like two million acres in the Highlands and Islands, Orkney and Shetland, are occupied by crofts. Each of these individual smallholdings may consist of several different parts. There will be arable ground near the house, most likely a share in hill grazings for sheep and cattle, and, in suitable areas, a share in a peat moss, which will – after a few weeks of very hard work – provide fuel for a whole year at no cost in cash.

Use of the common grazings around crofting villages, usually called townships, is arranged by an elected grazings committee. And much of the work at busy times is shared among neighbours. The general regulation of crofting, including transfers of land, loans and grants for improvements, is done by the Crofters Commission in Inverness.

Many crofters have full-time or part-time jobs elsewhere, perhaps in fishing or forestry, or work the crofts in retirement. Occasionally, a crofter will have amalgamated several smaller holdings into something nearer in size to a conventional farm.

A hospitable croft will provide ideal holiday accommodation, especially in districts off the beaten track.

A thatched crofthouse and (inset) the shaggy face of a Highland cow ▼

where the Forestry Commission's Glentarken walk wanders through old oakwoods above the village.

On the other side of the loch, a narrower road goes along the foot of the southern hills which soar up to the 3,224ft summit of Ben Vorlich. The gardens of Ardvorlich House, with many species of rhododendron growing in a glen, are occasionally open to the public. A hill-walker's track goes up Glen Ample, overlooked by the crags on the western outliers of Ben Vorlich, to cross a pass and then descend steeply through the forest plantations to Loch Lubnaig.

LOCH LOMOND

MAP REF: 91NS3598

Celebrated in a song which has spread far beyond the bounds of Scotland, Loch Lomond is the largest sheet of inland water in Britain, almost 23 miles from north to south. The northern part of the loch is a narrow cleft between high mountains. The southern part is totally different, fanning out in a spread of richly-wooded islands.

This is recreational water. The tangle of islands makes Loch Lomond an ideal sailing, motor-boating, canoeing, water-skiing and sail-boarding area. Game-fishermen set out to catch salmon, sea trout and brown trout. There is coarse angling, too, for pike and perch, roach and eels, although – as on Loch Eck – little chance to catch the elusive powan, the fresh-water herring.

From the south, Loch Lomond is approached by the A82 from Glasgow. A detour has to be made to reach Balloch, the village at the head of the River Leven, which acts as the gateway to Loch Lomond.

Main picture: the wooded banks of Loch Lomond seen from Balmaha, on the eastern shore ▼

Inset: looking across Loch Maree to the impressive peak of Slioch ▼

At Balloch the Leven is crowded with boatyards, and this is where many of the loch cruises start. On the east bank is Balloch Park, with woods and meadows and riverside walks. There is a nature trail through the park, a visitor centre, and, hidden away unexpectedly at the heart of it, a quiet walled garden.

The A82 reaches the lochside at Duck Bay, where a bypassed stretch of the main road has been retained as another picnic area. Offshore is Inchmurrin, biggest of Loch Lomond's islands, with a farm and some holiday houses, and a hotel with its own private ferry. The most impressive feature of the view is the wedged summit of Ben Lomond, 3192ft high and the most southerly mountain over 3000ft in Scotland.

Luss is the picturebook village of Loch Lomondside, mostly Victorian cottages with roses round the doors, and a main street that leads to a shingle bay and a rebuilt pier. There is an attractive parish church of 1875, with many earlier relics, on a rise of ground above the sparkling Luss Water. Between the church and the main road is the field where Luss Highland Games are held every July.

The next village on the lochside is Inverbeg. It has a hotel, an art gallery, a camping and caravan site, and a summer passenger ferry to Rowardennan at the foot of Ben Lomond.

Loch Lomond becomes narrower as you travel north. Alongside the 'narrows' of the loch, the A82 twists along a wooded hillside to the road-junction village of Tarbet, built round a typically Victorian hotel.

A narrow and winding stretch of the A82, through lochside woods, leads to the bridge at Inveruglas, where generations of travellers have kept a lookout for the tree on the left side 'growing out of a rock'. The bare hills beyond the boundary of the Inveruglas Water are the catchment area for the Loch Sloy hydroelectric scheme. Sadly, the huge pipes which bring the water downhill to the turbines of the lochside power station are all too visible. Near here is a lochside car park with a picnic area and a much more natural viewpoint.

Beyond Inveruglas the main road winds through open country to Ardlui. The West Highland Railway, within earshot from Tarbet, is now more clearly in view. There is a station at Ardlui, caravan and camping sites, and a pier.

Returning to Balloch and taking the A811 north-east towards Drymen leads to the village of Gartocharn. A side-road to the right after Gartocharn Hotel goes to the start of a short but steep footpath to the summit of Duncryne. This hill is a 360-degree viewpoint, but the greatest attraction is the panorama of Loch Lomond, the wooded islands and the mountains piling up on the

northern skyline.

In Drymen, a dead-end road turns off to the left of Balmaha, the main village on the eastern shore of the loch. Balmaha has a busy boatyard, from which visitors can be ferried to the nature reserve island of Inchcailloch just offshore. A nature trail has been laid out across its oak-covered hillsides, leading past the ruins of a 12th-century church and churchyard.

From the large car park at Balmaha a gentle walk leads through low-lying plantations. A much steeper route climbs through larch woods to a series of hilltop viewpoints, then down to the water's edge at Balmaha pier.

Northwards, the road wanders past farms, forests and camping and caravan sites among the lochside oakwoods. There are parking and picnic places by the gravelly shore or beside the rocks of some more rugged inlets, and forest trails at Sallochy and Blair.

As well as these out-and-back walks, the eastern shore of Loch Lomond is also on the route of the West Highland Way, Scotland's first long-distance footpath, which heads north all the way to Fort William.

The public road ends at Rowardennan, beside another extensive car park and picnic area among the woodlands at the very foot of Ben Lomond. The main Ben Lomond footpath starts here.

From Rowardennan the West Highland Way leads north for seven miles to Inversnaid, last of the Loch Lomond villages. Reaching Inversnaid by car is a much more roundabout process, by way of Drymen, Aberfoyle, Loch Ard and Loch Arklet.

Just beyond the west end of Loch Arklet is Garrison of Inversnaid – its name unusually aggressive for just a cluster of farm buildings near a primary school. But there was once a garrison here, a Government barracks built in Jacobite days. The soldiers had a hard time of it, though, because the country around Inversnaid was controlled by Rob Roy MacGregor, who was not only an outlaw and cattle-raider, but also a Jacobite supporter.

Down at the lochside, Inversnaid itself is a tiny hamlet beside an old coaching hotel. It has an almost microscopic harbour from which a summer ferry sails to the west shore near Tarbet. The tumbling falls of the Snaid Burn are crossed by a high footbridge which leads south on to the Rowardennan stretch of the West Highland Way.

North of Inversnaid, the Way continues across difficult country to Glen Falloch. But Inversnaid does not insist on energetic pursuits. It is also a place to potter around, admiring the mountains, the falls, the harbour and the loch waters lapping against the rocky shore.

LOCH MAREE
MAP REF: 84NG9370

For many well-travelled visitors, this is the most beautiful inland loch in Scotland. Loch Maree has superb mountain scenery in the roadless wilderness north and east. On the south-west side, the mountains start with the 10,500-acre Beinn Eighe National Nature Reserve above the A832 Kinlochewe-Gairloch road.

The reserve's visitor centre at Aultroy is between Kinlochewe and the head of Loch Maree. Two fine nature trails start from a lochside picnic site two miles farther on. One reaches 350ft and the other 1800ft.

The classic low-level view in the district is from Bridge of Grudie, across the loch to the splendidly-proportioned peak of Slioch. Beyond Bridge of Grudie the road continues to Talladale, where the views over the loch, this time, are directly to its scattering of wooded islands. A short forest walk leads to the Victoria Falls, named after a royal visit in 1877.

At Slattadale, the Forestry Commission has laid out a car park and picnic site. This is also the start of a five-mile cross-country walk.

LOCH NESS

MAP REF: 87NH5223

Never mind that its peat-dark waters, impenetrable by even the most powerful submarine light, never freeze; that it is more than 20 miles long, is rarely more than a mile in width, and plunges to a greatest recorded depth of almost 1000ft. The single most important statistic about Loch Ness is that its unexplorable depths may be the home of some so-far unidentified 'monster'.

Going north-east from Fort William, the A82 reaches the head of the loch at Fort Augustus. A bridge in the centre of the village takes the main road over the Caledonian Canal, which joins Loch Ness here. In parkland by the lochside is St Benedict's Abbey, built in the 1880s around a fragment of the Hanoverian fort which gave the village its name. The Abbey is now a boys' school.

The A82 continues along the lochside to Invermoriston, Lewiston and Drumnadrochit. Before Lewiston is the memorial to John Cobb, that most gentlemanly of record-breakers, who was killed on the loch in 1952 in his jet-powered boat *Crusader*.

Also on the lochside is the substantial ruin of the mainly 16th-century Urquhart Castle, once the home of the chiefs of Clan Grant. It is open to the public.

In Lewiston, a side-road to the left leads towards a forest walk through oakwoods to the waterfalls on the Divach Burn. At Drumnadrochit, there are *two* Loch Ness Monster exhibitions, almost next door to

▲ Urquhart Castle on Loch Ness.
Inset: 'Nessie' at her exhibition
site

each other. They are both well worth visiting.

From Drumnadrochit the A82 follows the lochside and then the River Ness into Inverness. A more dramatic drive from Fort Augustus is to take the A862 which turns right before St Benedict's Abbey, then climbs steeply over the hills to Loch Tarff and Whitebridge. Beyond Whitebridge the B852 turns off to the left near a lonely church, winding down through birchwoods and heather to the two-part village of Foyers.

Opposite the post office in Upper Foyers, a footpath leads sharply down through the woods to a viewpoint looking directly across to the Falls of Foyers, as they plummet into a dark rock pool below. Lower Foyers is down a minor road to the left, and overlooks the shore of Loch Ness.

The unexpected size of these twin hillside villages is explained by the fact that, in the 1890s, Britain's first aluminium works was established here. Power was generated by a pioneering industrial hydroelectric scheme which diverted the waters of the falls. Curiously enough, the abbot of St Benedict's had set up a smaller-scale generating scheme here just a few years earlier.

Beyond Foyers is Inverfarigaig, a hamlet on a ledge above the loch. To the right, the first side-road leads into the constricted Pass of Inverfarigaig. Forest plantations climb steeply on one side, facing beetling rocky crags across a deep-set burn. Farigaig Forest Centre, in the Pass, is the start of a strenuous forest trail.

The second road to the right off the B852 is one of the most astonishing in the Highlands. It suddenly corkscrews up a dizzy hillside of birches, heather and rocky outcrops, emerging after six formidable hairpin bends in half a mile near a magnificent viewpoint high above Loch Ness, from which an imaginative visitor can ponder over the mysteries far below.

LOCH TAY

MAP REF: 92NN7040

Fifteen miles long, surrounded by hillsides and forests, Loch Tay has the A827 from Killin to Kenmore above its northern shore, and a pleasant minor road taking the southern route. At the head of the loch, Killin is well known for its dramatic south-western approach, as the A827 runs alongside the rock-slabs, whirlpools, pine-clad islands and miniature cascades of the Falls of Dochart, before crossing the River Dochart into the main street.

Killin has the air of a mountain

◀ The Falls of Dochart form an alluring scene and are a popular attraction for visitors to Killin village, dominated from the north-east by the peaks of the Tarmachans and beyond them, the 3984ft bulk of Ben Lawers. It has a good range of hotels, boarding-houses and shops.

Just after Edramucky Bridge, a narrow side-road turns steeply uphill to tackle the pass between the Tarmachans and Ben Lawers.

At Fearnan, the A827 comes down to the lochside. A side-road to the left leads towards the entrance to Glen Lyon – the longest glen in Scotland – and the village of Fortingall, well-known for the ancient yew in the parish churchyard, perhaps the oldest living thing in Britain, and for the legend that Pontius Pilate was born here while his father was helping to patrol the borders of the Roman Empire.

Kenmore is one of the most beautifully situated villages in Scotland. Rustic cottages line the short street from the parish church overlooking Loch Tay to the imposing gateway to the grounds of Taymouth Castle, once the seat of the Earls and Marquesses of Breadalbane. The village inn was built in 1572 and claims to be the oldest in Scotland. Robert Burns visited it during his Highland tour in 1787, and verses he wrote about Kenmore are preserved on a chimney-piece.

Busiest day of the year in Kenmore is 15 January, the ceremonial opening of the Tay salmon season. The River Tay, which flows eastwards out of the loch under a well-preserved bridge dating from 1774, continues past an 18-hole parkland golf course towards the rapids of Grandtully.

The other road from Killin to Kenmore, along the south side of the loch, goes through Ardeonaig and Ardtalnaig – two more angling centres – and the one-time mill village of Acharn.

A farm track which goes uphill beside the rebuilt mill provides a pleasant walk to the hidden Falls of Acharn. These are reached by a tunnel built through a ridge of ground to the left of the track. Inside the tunnel, the right fork leads to a well-placed belvedere (a raised turret) looking directly across a heavily-wooded glen to the falls.

In Victorian days, when visitors were escorted here, the idea was that the guide, walking politely behind them, would slip along the left-hand fork and suddenly reappear, with fiendish yells, leaping on to the viewpoint wall. Few visitors escaped without a moment of terror that the wild Highlanders were coming to get them!

LOCHINVER

MAP REF: 84NC0922

Although it is the home port of a commercial fishing fleet, an angling centre and the base for boat trips to the islands of Enard Bay, Lochinver is dominated by the inland deer-forest mountains of Assynt. From the west side of the village at Baddidarrach, the view over Lochinver and the houses along the shore road has the 'sugar loaf' summit of Suilven looming on the skyline.

From Ledmore to Lochinver, the main A837 is a modern road through wild and timeless scenery. The mountains of Quinag and Canisp tower above, as it goes through the angling resort of Inchnadamph and along the north side of Loch Assynt. There is a 3200-acre nature reserve at Inchnadamph, and the limestone beds on which this prodigious mountain landscape is based are shown clearly on the face of the 300ft cliffs at Stronchrubie, by the roadside before the village.

The main road into Lochinver from the east is a well engineered one, but a more dramatic approach – from the driver's point of view – is the narrow and twisting minor road from the south. Around Inverkirkaig it gives widespread seaward views.

Water and hills combine to give a classic Highland scene by Loch Tay ▼

HAGGIS

Contrary to popular belief south of the border, haggis is not shot seasonally on the moors; this greatest of Scottish savouries is the result of painstaking culinary expertise.

Although generally regarded as Scotland's national dish, haggis was, in fact, also common in England until the 18th century; thereafter its popularity waned. Was it perhaps that the Sassenachs came to learn of its innermost secrets? It has to be said that the ingredients of what Robert Burns described as the 'great chieftain o' the puddin' race' do not make pleasant reading for the squeamish.

Haggis is made from the heart, lungs and liver of a sheep, all finely chopped, combined with suet, onions, oatmeal, black pepper, salt, herbs and either vinegar or lemon juice. The mixture is sewn up in a sheep's cleaned and pre-boiled stomach bag and then boiled for about three hours. The bag has to be pricked here and there with a darning needle as soon as it starts to swell to prevent it from exploding – with the obvious consequences.

The tasty dish is served hot from the pot with neeps and tatties (turnips and potatoes) and, traditionally, washed down with neat whisky. On festive occasions, such as St Andrew's Night celebrations and especially Burns Suppers in January, the haggis is majestically piped into the dining room by a resplendently-clad Scottish piper.

Haggis: a dish to be savoured ▼

▲ The harbour at Mallaig is always busy with fishing boats

MACDUFF

MAP REF: 89NJ7064

Macduff, on the opposite side of the Deveron estuary from Banff, is the main fishing port on this stretch of coast, as well as a holiday resort. It has a fleet of seine-net fishing boats and its own quayside market.

While the harbour activity can be watched at close quarters, there is a higher-level viewpoint in front of the hillside Doune church, beside a massive anchor claimed to be from a wrecked ship of the Spanish Armada.

At the foot of the cliffs east of the town, the open-air Tarlair swimming pool has been a popular bathing place for many years.

Like Banff, Macduff offers angling on the Deveron, and a pleasant walk through Montcoffer Wood, high above the river, meets up with the west-bank path from Duff House at the Bridge of Alvah.

MALLAIG

MAP REF: 86NM6796

This is the end of the Road to the Isles. Mallaig is the terminal for the car-ferry to Armadale on Skye. Other ferries leave for the islands of Rum, Eigg, Muck and Canna, and for Inverie on Loch Nevis, the only village in the remote district of Knoydart, which has no road connection with the rest of mainland Scotland. Mallaig is also the western terminus of the West Highland Railway. The bustling fishing-boat quays are well worth visiting.

Two villages south of Mallaig are holiday resorts. Arisaig is built round a series of bays, with breathtaking views over the sea to the mountains of Skye and Rum. Morar is famous

The islands of Eigg (centre) and Rum seen from near Mallaig ▶

for its white sandy beaches. Loch Morar, behind the village, is the deepest inland water in Britain – and the reputed home of Morag, a mysterious creature not unlike the monster of Loch Ness.

THE MEARNS

MAP REF: 89NO6274

Between the foothills of the Grampians and the North Sea, the heart of the Mearns is a landscape of rich farmlands and wooded estates. Laurencekirk is the main, but small-scale, inland market town, once famous for the snuff-boxes which are now valuable collectors' pieces.

On the edge of the hills, close to the line of the Highland Boundary Fault, Fettercairn has a grand and unexpected Gothic archway entrance, commemorating the visit of Queen Victoria and Prince Albert in 1861.

North of the village, the mansion-house of Fasque, home of the Gladstones, is open to visitors in

summer. Victoria's prime minister was one of the family.

Auchenblae is a hillside village with a pleasant riverbank 'den', a golf course, the preserved ruin of a 13th-century chapel and access to the forest walks in Drumtochty Glen.

Glenbervie churchyard is notable for the graves of Robert Burns' Mearns relations. Nearby, Drumlithie has an elegant little 18th-century steeple which once tolled the handloom weavers' hours.

A few miles down the winding course of the Bervie Water, the out-of-the-way parish church of St Ternan's Arbuthnott is one of the architectural glories of the Mearns, dating in part from 1242 and very carefully restored.

From the south, the coastal settlements start with St Cyrus, which has a cliff-edge nature reserve and a salmon-netting station. Johnshaven harbour now concentrates on shellfish, but whitefish auctions are still held every working day on the quayside at Gourdon, which also has facilities for sea angling.

Inverbervie has a figurehead memorial to the local man Hercules Linton, designer of the famous 19th-century tea-clipper *Cutty Sark*.

Kinneff's historic church was where the crown jewels of Scotland were hidden for years from Cromwell's troops. And gallery-goers all over Scotland know the clifftop village of Catterline, thanks to the landscape painting of Joan Eardley.

MOIDART

MAP REF: 90NM7075

At Inverailort on the Glenfinnan to Mallaig road the A861 turns south towards Kinlochmoidart. There are beautiful seaward views all the way down Loch Ailort to Glenuig.

A side-road to the right of Glenuig leads to the sheltered tidal bay of

WHISKY

A characteristic feature of many Highland valleys – in Speyside, Glenlivet, Perthshire and elsewhere – are the whitewashed buildings of malt whisky distilleries, with the pagoda-like roofs of their barley-drying kilns. Although there are many blended whiskies, connoisseurs prefer single malts, each of which comes from one particular distillery.

No two malt whiskies are identical, even when produced in distilleries only half a mile apart; and the taste, thanks to the water from the hill burns and springs, cannot be duplicated anywhere else in the world. Incidentally, this is the only case where the adjective Scotch is used instead of Scottish.

The first record of whisky distilling in Scotland is dated 1494. Imposition of excise duty in 1644 led to nearly two centuries of determined and profitable

▲ The malting house at the Glengarioch Distillery at Oldmeldrum

smuggling. The business settled down to its modern form after a more reasonable Act of Parliament in 1823.

There are more than 100 malt whisky distilleries in the Highlands and Islands. Many of them offer guided tours to demonstrate the carefully-timed processes involved

in producing what Gaelic speakers call *uisge-beatha* – the water of life. Six of the Speyside distilleries lie on the 'Whisky Trail'; this is a signposted road tour some 70 miles long. Allow about an hour for each distillery visit, but make sure that only car passengers do the sampling.

Samalaman. From there, a footpath goes over a pass to the one-time crofting settlement of Smearisary, looking out over the sea to Eigg.

From Glenuig the A861 goes over the shoulder of a hill and down again to Kinlochmoidart. Bonnie Prince Charlie stayed at Kinlochmoidart House in 1745, on his way to the raising of the Jacobite standard at Glenfinnan.

Midway down Loch Moidart, reached by a side-road off the A861, the ruin of Castle Tioram is one of the great sights of the coast. It was the fortress of the MacDonalds of Clanranald, built on a rock at the end of a natural causeway, which allows it to be reached on foot at low tide.

MONTROSE
MAP REF: 93NO7157

This attractive Angus town spreads north from the docks at the narrow mouth of the River South Esk - busy with cargo ships, fishing boats and North Sea oil work; but immediately inland the river has created a vast tidal basin which dries out almost completely at low water. Montrose Basin is a nature reserve, a fine place for observing pinkfoot and greylag geese, wigeon and redshank.

The town centre has many attractive older buildings, some of them originally town mansions of wealthy landed families. East of the main street there is a district with a notably spacious and elegant air.

Montrose museum is strong on relics of the old whaling industry,

Pictish stones and locally-gathered collections of fossils and agates.

The built-up area does not encroach on the Links, where golf courses are laid out behind the dunes which border the long stretches of sandy beach.

NAIRN
MAP REF: 85NH8756

With its situation beside the sea, its natural links-land turf, and one of the mildest and driest climates in Scotland, it is not surprising that Nairn developed into a well-known golfing resort. The main part of the town, however, is built back from the Moray Firth, around the A96 Inverness to Forres road. There are walks by the shore and along the

A creel finds an alternative use on a house in Nairn's fishertown ▼

banks of the River Nairn. The Constabulary Garden, open daily from May to September, is a pleasant town-centre retreat.

At Viewfield House there is a local history museum with a display on the Battle of Culloden; and the days when Nairn was a premier fishing port are recalled in the Fishertown Museum in King Street.

South-west of Nairn, off the B9090, Cawdor Castle is the most famous stately home in the district. Macbeth was Thane of Cawdor in Shakespeare's play, but the existing building is of much later date. The 14th-century castle, home of the present-day Earl of Cawdor, is open daily from May to October. Attractions include not only tours of the castle itself, in its fine setting among gardens and woodland on the banks of a rocky burn, but also a network of varied nature trails.

NEWBURGH

MAP REF: 93NO2318

Anglers often come to Newburgh to fish the tidal waters of the narrow and winding estuary of the River Ythan for sea trout and salmon. There is also a peninsula golf course at the start of the 12-mile stretch of beach, extending all the way south to Aberdeen.

Across the Ythan is one of the most remarkable nature reserves in Scotland. The Sands of Forvie reserve – linked with another which includes the estuary itself – covers a huge area of sand dunes, cliffs and tidal shore.

This is Britain's largest nesting site for eider ducks, and there are also great numbers of geese, waders and terns.

A waymarked path leads over tussocky heathland to the ruined parish church of Forvie, all that remains above ground of a village abandoned to the encroaching sandhills, and then follows the shore north towards the village of Collieston.

OBAN

MAP REF: 90NM8630

Built round a curving bay, sheltered by the long island of Kerrera from the open waters of the Firth of Lorn, Oban is a holiday resort with many seafront hotels, as well as a trading and transport centre. It is the terminus of the West Highland railway from Glasgow, and the Railway Pier, busy with fishing boats unloading their catches, is the start of many car-ferry routes, to Mull, Coll and Tiree, Barra and South Uist, Colonsay and the nearer island of Lismore. There are cruises to Iona, and local boat-hirers run excursions to smaller islets which are breeding grounds of seals.

South of the harbour, there are walks on Pulpit Hill, past the wooded grounds of well-placed Victorian villas to a viewpoint on the summit. Directly inland, the skyline is marked by McCaig's Tower, a folly built in the 1890s to provide work at a time of depression. This near-replica of the Colosseum in Rome is a place for marvellous westward views.

Oban Bay is a fine sailing area. Sea-anglers have marks off Kerrera. Loch and river fishermen have plenty of choice inland, such as the trout and salmon beats of Loch Scammadale and the River Euchar which flows from it to join the sea at Kilninver, on the A816 south of the town.

Oban has an 18-hole golf course in a wooded setting in Glencruitten.

Shinty is a favourite game here. And Oban Highland Games – otherwise known as the Argyllshire Gathering – are a notable sporting and social event in August.

North of the bay, a road above the shore leads to Ganavan Sands. This is Oban's swimming and sun-bathing centre, with an abundance of parking space and a caravan site attached.

The easiest island to reach from Oban is Kerrera, a fine place for a day's outing. Along Gallanach Road there is parking space beside the jetty from which the ferry makes its five-minute crossing. A circular walk of about six miles can be followed on Kerrera, on farm tracks and

▲ Sunset over Oban highlights the outline of McCaig's Tower

footpaths, past the ruins of the 16th-century Gylen Castle. The wild scenery and the sense of away-from-it-all are matched by the varied seaward views.

South of Oban, a turning off the A816 near Kilninver leads on to the B844 which crosses the high-arched Clachan Bridge – optimistically called 'the bridge over the Atlantic' – up to the island of Seil. Ellanbeich on the west coast is a one-time slate-quarriers' village turned into a neatly whitewashed holiday centre. The sheltered garden of An Cala is open on Monday and Thursday afternoons from April to September. A ferry crosses to the smaller slate island of Easdale, which has its own folk museum.

Back on the mainland, beyond the golf course at Glencruitten, a minor road to the south goes alongside Loch Nell to rejoin the A816 near the head of Loch Feochan. Farther east, the road through Glen Lonan

passes Barguillean, where a lochside garden is open daily from April to October.

Northwards, the A85 leads to Connel, on the south shore of Loch Etive at the Falls of Lora – the tide-race under the former railway bridge which takes the A826 into the districts of Benderloch and Barcaldine. Off the A826 there are forest walks, one leading to the 1,010ft summit of Beinn Lora.

The Sea Life Centre, before the village of Barcaldine, is open from March to November. Tanks contain displays of all kinds of fish, from rays and octopus to turbot and eels. And a twice-daily attraction is the seal feeding in the open-air pool.

Turning off to the right at Barcaldine, the B845 goes up through the forest plantations of Gleann Salach then down to the shore of Loch Etive and an unexpectedly industrial-looking quarry village.

The road then wanders along the north shore of Loch Etive, back to the bridge at Connel, passing Ardchattan Priory. This is a private house, based on a ruined 13th-century Benedictine priory, and can be visited on occasional summer Sundays.

The main attraction at Ardchattan, however, is the garden, open daily from April to October. Its herbaceous borders and flowering shrubs are a reminder that there are attractive miniature landscapes around Oban, as well as the grander-scale mountains, forests, sea-lochs and islands offshore.

THE INNER ISLES

THE MAGIC ISLANDS

The Inner Hebridean islands, easily accessible from the mainland, have much to offer in scenery, wildlife, history and the indefinable feeling of magic that islands always carry.

Mull is just a 40-minute ferry ride from Oban, with six crossings a day in the summer. The ferry docks at Craignure, from where a pleasant 30-minute walk leads to Torosay Castle. Alternatively, you can get there on the charming Mull Railway, a narrow-gauge line with a character all of its own. Torosay has many interesting exhibits and a large garden displaying a line of Italian statuary.

Just across the bay from Torosay is Duart Castle, home of the chiefs of the Clan Maclean. It was started in the 13th century and has a commanding position guarding the Sound of Mull. The castle was forfeited by the clan chief in 1745 and not recovered until 1911 when Sir Fitzroy Maclean began its restoration.

The A849 heads west through Glen More to the Ross of Mull. A minor road from Pennyghael leads down to Carsaig, from where an adventurous walk takes you to Carsaig Arches, a natural rock formation in the cliffs. Back on the main road, there are fine views across Loch Scridain to the cliffs of Ardmeanach. The road ends at Fionnphort for the short ferry across to Iona.

Now owned by the National Trust for Scotland, St Columba's island retains a distinctly peaceful

atmosphere. The superb abbey dates originally from the 13th century and is the home of the Iona Community, founded by Dr George Macleod (now Lord Macleod of Fuinary) in 1938. The Reilig Orain, said to be the burial ground of 48 Scottish kings, can also be seen.

North of Craignure, the A849 leads past Salen to Tobermory and its bay; a town of attractive houses painted in bright colours. There are woodland walks south of the town and also at Aros. The B8073 makes a circuit of the northern part of Mull to arrive at Dervaig, where the Mull Little Theatre, renowned as Britain's smallest with only 43 seats, can be found together with the Old Byre, a visitor centre with displays on the history and wildlife of the island.

The road continues to Calgary, superbly sited on its bay with a wonderful beach. The city in Canada took its name from this lovely place. House of Treshnish is open daily from April to October and has fine walks through its woodlands, with wide views out to sea.

The road continues high above Loch Tuath (North Loch) with the island of Ulva offshore and runs along Loch na Keal, from where Ben More, the only peak on Mull over 3,000ft, can easily be seen, to rejoin the A849 at Salen.

THE SMALL ISLES

The four islands of Rum, Eigg, Canna and Muck are collectively called the Small Isles. They are served by regular ferry from Mallaig or can be visited on a day trip from Arisaig.

Rum, the largest of the four, is owned by Scottish Natural Heritage (previously the Nature Conservancy Council and Countryside Commission [Scotland]) and is run as a huge outdoor laboratory with experiments involving deer, native trees and above all the magnificent sea eagles, successfully reintroduced here in the past 20 years. Kinloch Castle, a wild architectural extravaganza built by Sir George Bullough, the Lancashire cotton magnate who owned the island in Victorian times, offers accommodation, but prior booking is essential as visitor numbers are, quite rightly, strictly controlled.

Canna has been owned by the National Trust for Scotland since 1981, gifted by the previous owner, the eminent Gaelic scholar Dr John Lorne Campbell, who still lives on the island. It is a flat, pastoral island 5 miles long and just over a mile across.

Eigg and Muck both support small communities. Eigg is dominated by the sharp prow of the Sgurr, the beetling cliff above its main bay. Both islands maintain a way of life that is precarious today but precious to those who live there.

COLL AND TIREE

A superb boat trip through the Sound of Mull from Oban takes you to Coll and Tiree, large treeless islands of distinct character. Both hide their best face – the wonderful western seaboard where the Atlantic waves crash in and the machair, the grassy dunes, support an unbelievably rich array of flowers in summer.

Tiree has become renowned as a venue for windsurfing, with major competitions held each autumn. Although roughly the same size as Coll, 12 miles long by three broad, it supports a population of nearly 1,000 whereas Coll has less than 200. Tiree has an airstrip and a golf course.

There are remains of brochs on both islands, and a more recent castle at Breacachadh on Coll, a restored 15th-century tower house now owned by the Maclean-Bristol family and used for summer camps and courses.

There are many other islands which can be visited, such as Colonsay, Islay and Jura, but which we have no space for here. The exploration of 'offshore Scotland' is immensely rewarding, and modern ferry services make travelling much easier than it formerly was. Information can be obtained at all the main ports such as Oban and Mallaig.

Brightly painted houses line the harbour front at Tobermory, principal town on the island of Mull ▼

OLDMELDRUM

MAP REF: 82NJ8027

A high-set town in the heart of extensive farming country, Oldmeldrum lies on the borders of the old provinces of Formartine and Garioch and has an interesting conservation area around its Market Square. Glengarioch distillery on the outskirts is open to visitors, and has a notable reputation for energy conservation – its glasshouses producing a rich crop of tomatoes every year.

Five miles east, the National Trust for Scotland's splendid Great Garden of Pitmedden has been restored to its formal 17th-century style, and some of the estate buildings have been converted into a Museum of Farming Life.

North-east of Oldmeldrum is another major Trust property – the handsomely-furnished Haddo House, completed in 1732 for the Earl of Aberdeen. It is well known for its music society concerts.

The mansion house stands at the edge of Haddo Country Park, where nature trails explore the varied woodlands, the parkland, and the edges of a lake where tufted duck, moorhens and swans cruise in the summer.

Of the nearby villages, Tarves is a 19th-century conservation area in its own right; Methlick, with an imposing Victorian parish church, is an angling centre of the Upper Ythan.

PERTH

MAP REF: 92N01123

At its heart, Perth is a Georgian town, although St John's Kirk dates from the 15th century. John Knox's famous sermon here in May 1559 sparked off the Reformation in Scotland. The tourist information centre in High Street has leaflets

▲ The richly decorated State Bed is one of the historic attractions at regal Scone Palace, near Perth

outlining town walks which take in many historical sites, including the North and South Inches, two very large public spaces gifted to Perth in 1377. The North Inch has playing fields, a golf course, cricket pitch and on its western edge, the modern Bell's sports centre and Balhousie Castle, which holds the regimental museum of the Black Watch. The South Inch has boating, putting and play areas.

An intriguing walk from the South Inch leads across the River Tay to Moncrieffe Island, home of the King George IV golf club – unusual for being on an island and for having no vehicular access. Continuing across the river, you come to Branklyn Garden (NTS), famed for its rhododendrons and herbaceous borders. It is open from March to October. You can continue past Branklyn on to Kinnoull Hill and its well-known folly on the cliff edge, from where there is a superb view over the Tay to the hills of Fife.

On the west side of the town there is a splendid new leisure pool and ice rink and not far away, the Cherrybank Gardens, provided by Bell's Whisky, which contain

The Tay winds through Perth, under Smeaton's fine old bridge ▼

hundreds of different heathers and an attractive water garden with sculptures. A different kind of industry is found at Caithness Glass on the A9 just north of Perth, where you can watch glassblowing and visit an excellent souvenir shop.

Perth's museum and art gallery (open all year) has particularly good displays on the natural history of the area. A little north of Perth on the A93 is Scone Palace and its grounds, which include a pinetum and an adventure play area. The palace is open from Easter to October and has superb collections of furniture and porcelain. Scone was for centuries the coronation site of Scottish kings.

PITLOCHRY

MAP REF: 92NN9458

Set in one of the most beautiful valleys in the Central Highlands, Pitlochry is a holiday resort of hotels and boarding houses, with camping and caravan sites nearby, facilities for golf, angling and boating, an indoor sports centre and any number of exhilarating hill and forest walks.

The North of Scotland Hydro-Electric Board's reservoir of Loch Faskally has winding banks clothed in natural woodland. On the east side of the loch, a Forestry Commission trail goes through the woodland garden of a former private estate and round an ornamental lake.

At the south end of the loch there is a fish pass, with an observation room from which salmon can be seen battling their way upstream.

Pitlochry Festival Theatre has graduated from its original marquee of 1951 to a modern, purpose-built £2 million building – but it is still very much Scotland's 'theatre in the hills'.

Queen's View, lying north-west of Pitlochry, beside the B8019 which runs along the north side of Loch Tummel, is one of the most famous viewpoints in Scotland, and was so christened after Queen Victoria admired the view on an excursion in 1866. There is a Forestry Commission information centre open from Easter to September on one side of the road, and, on the other, forest walks climbing to more viewpoints, an excavated ring fort of the 8th or 9th century, and a reconstructed 18th-century farm village.

RANNOCH

MAP REF: 92NN6759

The B8019 meanders west from Pitlochry for nearly 40 miles, and after passing the Queen's View it

▲ Laggan Locks, Caledonian Canal

THE CALEDONIAN CANAL

On any map of Scotland, the eye is drawn naturally to the long line of the Great Glen, a vast natural fault created aeons ago, running south-west to north-east from Argyll to the Moray Firth. It holds Loch Lochy, Loch Oich and above all Loch Ness, and in the late 18th century it was realised that joining these lochs by canal would provide a relatively safe route cutting out the long and hazardous sea journey round the western and northern coasts of Scotland.

The great engineer Thomas Telford was given the task of bringing the canal to reality, and by spring 1804 its line had been decided and work commenced at either end. It was to take 18 years to complete, and there were many difficulties to overcome – not least the West Highland weather, and the intractable nature of some of the major landowners! Over 1,000 men were employed on the construction work, which went on all year round.

The full length of the canal was first sailed in October 1822, and since then it has provided passage for many thousands of vessels. Its principal use today is for leisure craft. There are flights of locks at Corpach (called Neptune's Staircase), Laggan, Fort Augustus and Inverness.

The canal offers many walking possibilities; its towpath and a former railway line can be followed for much of its length, and it is hoped that before long it will all be walkable under the name of the Great Glen Way. There are particularly good walks from Fort Augustus, Corpach and Laggan, and it is very pleasant to stroll along watching the small boats, and perhaps thinking of all the problems that had to be overcome before this extraordinary engineering feat was completed nearly 200 years ago.

Opposite the hamlet of Crathie on the A93, the B976 crosses the Dee and then turns back along the south bank towards Ballater, passing the main entrance to the castle. Visitors are welcome to the grounds and gardens, and to an exhibition in the castle ballroom, on weekdays from May to July when the Royal Family is not in residence.

Crathie is often jammed with sightseers when the Royal Family attend the little parish church, built in 1895 and open to visitors. Because the sparsely-populated parish found it hard to gather enough money for the building, a fund-raising bazaar was held in the grounds of Balmoral, with the full approval of Queen Victoria and with some of her family helping to run the stalls.

▲ Balmoral, Deeside's royal home

reaches Loch Tummel and the Tummel Forest Park, where many walks are available. Braes of Foss, south of the loch, is the normal start point for the ascent of Schiehallion, the conical mountain used by the Astronomer Royal, Nevil Maskelyne, in the 18th century, in experiments to determine the mass of the earth.

The road continues (now as B846) past Tummel Bridge and Dunalastair Water to Kinloch Rannoch, the main village for the area, before running for 10 miles beside Loch Rannoch. A minor road takes to the south side of the loch and offers more forest walks at Carie and in the Black Wood of Rannoch with its old Caledonian pine trees, one of the haunts of the capercaillie, Scotland's largest woodland bird. A marathon is run right round the loch each summer.

From Bridge of Gaur there are another six miles to Rannoch Station and its hotel, on the line to Fort William. Just north of here is one of the very few snow tunnels on any British rail line. If you want to continue westwards, across the wild expanse of Rannoch Moor, you must do so on foot. A long day's tramp of 15 miles would get you to Kingshouse Hotel in Glencoe: to reach the same point by car involves a tortuous journey of over 100 miles.

ROYAL DEESIDE
MAP REF: 89NO3095

Of all the rivers in Britain, the Dee rises highest in the mountains, bubbling up from the Wells of Dee, more than 4,000ft above sea level near Einich Cairn in the Cairngorms. From there it plunges down the cliffs of An Garbh Choire (the rough corrie) into the deep pass of the Lairig Ghru, and, gathering tributaries from either side, flows down into that area of pine woods (larch, birch and juniper), rocks and tumbling waters which make up the classic Deeside view.

Once past Braemar, the landscape takes in fields on the valley floor, plantations and natural woods sweeping up to heathery grouse moors and high, bare hills above. But what has made it famous is Balmoral Castle, the Royal Family's Highland home.

Queen Victoria and Prince Albert bought the estate in 1852 for £31,500, and then commissioned the Aberdeen city architect William Smith to build a new castle of local Glen Gelder granite. Many of the Prince's own ideas were incorporated into the design. Victoria and Albert were welcomed to their new Scottish home on 7 September 1855, and the future of Royal Deeside was assured.

Downstream of Ballater, as the A93 continues past Cambus o'May and on to the moors around Dinnet, it leaves the strictly Highland part of Royal Deeside. Muir of Dinnet is a National Nature Reserve comprising a wide expanse of heather, oakwood, birch, rowan and pines around Loch Davan and Loch Kinord. The Burn o'Vat is named after a huge rocky cauldron which can be visited from a car park on the A97.

Farther along the A93 is the attractive village of Aboyne, in a wooded setting with granite cottages and villas surrounding a large green, where Aboyne Highland Games are held each year in September.

A right turn along the B976 leads to Glen Tanar estate, where a visitor centre is open from April to September. It combines a wildlife and land-use exhibition, with fine woodland walks and a nature trail. Here in this side-valley, once again, are the elements of the classic Deeside landscape – a backdrop of hills with pine woods, heather and a river tumbling through a lovely glen.

SKYE

MAP REF: 86NG5030

The largest of Scotland's islands, Skye has a wild and mountainous interior, where the peaks, ridges and pinnacles of the Cuillin Hills are among the finest rock-climbing areas in Europe. The coastline, with all its indentations, is said to stretch for almost a thousand miles. In any description of Skye, take for granted a multiplicity of magnificent sea and mountain views.

The shortest sea-crossing to Skye is by car-ferry from Kyle of Lochalsh to Kyleakin, which takes its name from the Norse King Haakon. He sailed through this narrow straight on his way to defeat at the Battle of Largs in 1263. A toll-bridge is to be built here in the mid-1990s.

Kyle House gardens, beside the A850 as it leaves the village, are notable for their flowering shrubs and splendid coastal views. They are open to the public from May to August. Just offshore is Kyleakin Island. It was the home in 1968–9 of the author-naturalist Gavin Maxwell, after his original home *Camusfearna* on the mainland was burned down.

A side-road to the left goes up lonely Glen Arróch then dives down the far side of a pass to the remote village of Kylerhea, where a summer-only ferry operates to Glenelg. Opposite the Glen Arroch turning is the only airfield on Skye.

Beyond the crofting township of Breakish, where the old school is the printing works for the *West Highland Free Press* weekly newspaper, the A851 turns off across the moors to the peninsula of Sleat (pronounced Slate) in the south-eastern corner of Skye. The first village is the prosperous and neat-looking Isleornsay, sharing its name with a tidal island which, like the one off Kyleakin, was once owned by Gavin Maxwell.

Beyond Isleornsay the A851 continues to Ostaig, where a Gaelic college has been established, and then to Armadale, the port for the Mallaig car-ferry service. On this section of the Sleat peninsula is the impressive 17,000-acre MacDonald estate. Armadale Castle, set in 40 acres of woodland gardens and nature trails, is the Clan Donald Centre and museum, with the restored stables, dating from 1820,

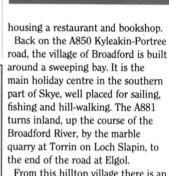

housing a restaurant and bookshop.

Back on the A850 Kyleakin-Portree road, the village of Broadford is built around a sweeping bay. It is the main holiday centre in the southern part of Skye, well placed for sailing, fishing and hill-walking. The A881 turns inland, up the course of the Broadford River, by the marble quarry at Torrin on Loch Slapin, to the end of the road at Elgol.

From this hilltop village there is an unparalleled view, across Loch Scavaig, to the serrated main ridge of the Cuillin Hills, the finest mountain skyline in Scotland, with a rim of summits over 3,000ft. There are cruises from Elgol to the head of Loch Scavaig, where the mountains sweep up directly from the sea.

Returning to Broadford and continuing on the A850, the road passes through forest plantations, past the sailing centre of Strollamus and the croft-house museum at Luib on the shore of Loch Ainort. The modern main road goes over an inland pass towards the hamlet of Sconser, but the old main road is still open, following the coast.

Sconser starts with Skye's only golf course, a nine-hole layout also grazed by sheep, and an 18th-century inn. On the shore of Loch Sligachan is the slipway for the car and passenger ferry to Raasay, a beautiful island of very pleasant forest, hill and moorland walks. There are many remains of Raasay's contribution to industrial archaeology – an ironstone mine worked from 1913–19, mostly by German prisoners-of-war, for whom

LIFE TODAY ON SKYE

Agriculture and tourism are the most important industries on Skye. There are over 1,800 crofts on the island but very few are able to support the families that own them and they are usually run as a sideline to supplement the income from other jobs. No-one lives far from the sea and many islanders have small boats for fishing. They put down pots to catch lobsters and crabs which they sell locally or send across to the mainland.

The small clusters of houses scattered over the island are called townships. In the little townships on the north-west, someone like the local postman could well have a croft of 20 acres with two cows and 100 or so sheep which also graze the common land. Crofters and their dogs know every sheep in their flock and can tell them apart from the thousands of others which roam the glen. The crofting year starts at the end of November, following the natural cycle of the sheep.

Unless crofters offer bed and breakfast their lives are largely unaffected by the considerable number of tourists who visit Skye each year. In the height of the season visitors can outnumber the resident population, which has fallen to about 6,000. In 1840,

23,000 people lived on Skye but lack of work forced them to emigrate to Australia, New Zealand and America. Now, many MacDonalds, MacLeods, MacKenzies and Macphersons return as tourists from these countries 'over the sea to Skye' looking for their roots.

An increasing number of settlers coming to the island are English, drawn by the calm lifestyle and magnificent scenery. They bring skills or offer special services like study holidays for amateur naturalists and organised climbing in the Cuillins. Craftsmen make fine products of every variety, selling them from small studios attached to their workshops.

Winters can be hard and very windy in the remoter areas. A storm may cut off electricity for several days so households have to be self-sufficient, but the peace and the beauty of the snow-clad hills help to compensate for any inconvenience.

Although some hotels close during the winter, tradesmen, like hairdressers, who cater for the tourists during the season find themselves busy with local trade. Wedding and club dinners normally take place during winter months when residents are able to have the Island and its facilities to themselves.

▲ The sharp outline of the Cuillin Hills seen from Sligachan; on the right is Sgurr nan Gillean (peak of the young men)

the village of Inverarish was originally built.

Back on Skye, beyond the head of Loch Sligachan, with a splendid mountain background, stands the isolated Sligachan Hotel, the major peak of Sgurr nan Gillean rising to the south. This is one of Skye's rock-climbing and hill-walking centres, with trout and salmon in the river nearby.

The A850 goes north of Sligachan by way of Glen Varrigill, where there is a forest walk in the roadside plantations, to Portree, the island's capital. Portree has a fishing-boat harbour at the head of a sheltered bay, a wide selection of hotels and boarding-houses, opportunities for sailing, fishing and walking.

From Portree the A850 cuts diagonally across the island, through Skeabost and Edinbane to the village of Dunvegan. It finishes near Dunvegan Castle, set among woodlands and gardens on one side, on a rock above its sea-loch on the other. This is the most-visited place on Skye, the home for 700 years of the MacLeods of Dunvegan, chiefs of the clan. The castle and its grounds are open on weekdays from Easter to October. There are boat trips, in season, to the island breeding grounds of the grey seals.

Back at Portree, the main road round the north end of Skye is the A855. It runs along the coast below the mountain ridge of Trotternish, with the isolated rock tower called the Old Man of Storr clearly in view.

A forest walk runs through the plantations here.

At Invertote, a minor road turns inland to the abandoned rock workings at Loch Cuithir, alongside the remains of the mineral railway which took supplies to the coast. North of Invertote, a car park and viewpoint by the edge of a cliff near Elishader look north to the Kilt Rock, given that name because the basalt columns, rising above the sea, look like the pleats of a kilt.

Round the north end of the island, the main road passes close to Duntulm Castle, a ruined clifftop fortress once held by the MacDonald Lords of the Isles. South of Duntulm is the scattered village of Kilmuir. One group of roadside houses has been turned into the Skye Cottage Museum, open on weekdays from May to September.

The most famous place of pilgrimage at Kilmuir is the graveyard on a side-road to the left. Flora MacDonald, the great heroine of the Jacobites, is buried here. In the dark days after the Battle of Culloden in 1746, when Prince Charles Edward Stuart was being hunted by Government troops and informers, she smuggled him across from Lewis to Skye, disguised as her maid.

Spread around a bay, Uig is an important link in the Hebridean ferry services. A car-ferry sails from here to Tarbert in Harris and Lochmaddy in North Uist. Some of the most adventurous motoring on

Skye is along a hill road from Uig, across the middle of the Trotternish peninsula towards Staffin, hairpinning down a pass beside the rocky pinnacles of the Quiraing.

Back on the moorlands near Portree, the A856 which leads south from Uig meets up with the A850 Dunvegan road. South of Dunvegan, the B884 wanders into the peninsula between Loch Dunvegan and Loch Bracadale and on to Glendale. This, like so much of Skye, is an area with plenty to see: an art gallery, a pottery, the Skye Black House Museum, silver and knitwear workshops, and a restored 18th-century water-mill.

In 1904, after leading the movement for land reform, the people of Glendale became the first crofter-landlords in Scotland. The single-track road continues past Waterstein, where a Field Studies Centre offers nature study holidays, to Neist Point. A walk out to the lighthouse is rewarded by magnificent panoramic views of the Outer Islands.

Avoiding the turn-off, the rebuilt A863 Dunvegan–Sligachan road goes by Bracadale, past the loop-roads to Harlosh and its sub-aqua diving centre, and to Ullinish. At the head of Loch Harport the B8009 turns off to Carbost and the Talisker distillery, the only one on the island.

Off to the left of the B8009, before Carbost, another side-road winds over the moors and through forest plantations to Glenbrittle, the most famous rock-climbing centre on Skye, dominated to the east by the main Cuillin ridge. The highest summit is Sgurr Alasdair, almost 3,300ft high. It was first climbed in 1873 by Sheriff Alexander Nicholson, from whom it takes its name. Alasdair is the Gaelic form of Alexander.

The Cuillin ridge is for rock-climbers. It is not at all the place for a casual stroll. But there is a Forestry Commission picnic site by the roadside in the glen, placed so that it offers spectacular mountain views. Lesser mortals can sit quietly there and reflect on the remarkable variety of mountain and coastal scenery on Skye; on its climbing, angling, walking and sailing facilities; on its many craft workshops; on its history and its wildlife – golden eagles, sea-bird colonies, and rare alpine plants growing in remote corries and cliff edges.

Skye has been called the Winged Island, from its shape; the Misty Isle, from its mountain weather; and – as Sheriff Nicolson himself put it – the Queen of all the Isles.

61

▲ The lovely small harbour at Stonehaven, Grampian

STONEHAVEN

MAP REF: 89NO8685

Now bypassed by the main Aberdeen road, so that heavy traffic no longer rumbles through the main street of its 18th- and 19th-century town centre, Stonehaven is a well-equipped coastal holiday resort, with sandy beaches along its curving bay.

The fishing town on the south side is built beside a substantial harbour – a good sailing and sea angling base – with a quarter-circle of towering cliffs bending to a rocky point. The restored tolbooth on the way to the harbour now houses a local-history museum.

Among Stonehaven's many festivals and sporting events, the annual RW Thomson Memorial Run for vintage and veteran cars makes the point that the real inventor of the pneumatic tyre – years before Mr Dunlop – was a local man.

Two miles south, on a tremendous clifftop site, the partly-restored Dunnottar Castle is open to visitors. From here the crown jewels of Scotland were smuggled out during a siege by Cromwell's troops, to be hidden under the floor of the church at Kinneff. A fine clifftop walk leads from the town to the castle, or you can drive there.

STRATHDON

MAP REF: 89NJ3513

The River Don rises in the lonely hill country beyond the Lecht Road – the A939 from Cock Bridge to Tomintoul, usually the first road in

▲ Racing cars at the Grampian Transport Museum in Alford

the Highlands to be closed by winter blizzards. Dominating the valley above Cock Bridge is the restored 16th-century Corgarff Castle with its star-shaped ramparts and memories of a violent past. It is open daily from April to September.

Below Corgarff the course of the Don, as it winds through a now-forested valley, is followed by the B973 and then the A97, into the plain east of Kildrummy.

The original Kildrummy Castle was built in the 13th century, and its high-standing ruin, open daily throughout the year, is one of the most complete of its era. The present Kildrummy Castle, now a hotel, was built in 1900. The area from which the stones for it were quarried forms a Japanese water garden and an alpine garden, open from April to October. There is also a small museum.

Farther down the valley of the Don, Alford on the A944 is the site of the Grampian Transport Museum and of a railway museum incorporated in the old main-line station. Both are open from April to September. The station is now the terminus of the narrow-gauge Alford Valley Railway which runs via the Transport Museum into the two country parks of Haughton House and Murray Park, where there are nature trails and picnic sites. The railway operates scheduled services during the months when the museums are open.

STRATHPEFFER

MAP REF: 84NH4858

This was the most northerly of all Britain's spa resorts, based on the local sulphur and chalybeate springs. Most of the development took place in Victorian times, leaving Strathpeffer with a fine selection of hotels, some having a decidedly Continental look. Although the main spa buildings have gone, the pavilion and the pump room have been preserved. The old railway station has been rebuilt as a centre for craft businesses and an information office.

On the west side, Strathpeffer climbs a ridge with pleasant woodland walks, then dips down again to an energetic golf course. Knock Farril, the corresponding ridge to the east, has more footpaths, including one to an extensive hilltop viewpoint south over the wooded islands of Loch Ussie and north to the 3,433ft bulk of Ben Wyvis.

The two-mile stretch of the A832 north-west of Contin, a short drive from Strathpeffer, leads to Forestry Commission picnic sites in the larch woods by the Blackwater River and among the birches which fringe the beautiful and tranquil Loch Achilty. There are two forest walks from the Blackwater picnic site. Farther upstream, footpaths lead through woodlands to the salmon leap at the Falls of Rogie.

▲ The Falls of Rogie, near the village of Strathpeffer, are fed by the Blackwater, a fine salmon river, and form an impressive sight in spate

HIGHLAND CLANS

The word 'clan' is from the Gaelic *clann* meaning children and, in a sense, the Highland clansmen were part of individual great families in that they carried the same name, wore the same plaid, lived in the same area and owed loyalty to the same chief. To a large degree territorial boundaries frequently defined the bounds of clanship. For example, the Clan MacNeil territory was enclosed by the sea, and tall mountains were the defence lines of the Macdonalds of Glencoe. Within those boundaries the chief ruled his own clan and looked after their needs; in exchange the clansmen worked for him and fought for him in time of unrest. It was a patriarchal quasi-feudal system which worked well despite occasional internecine feuding. And it was only when central government, in the shape of successive Scottish and, latterly, British monarchs, began to intervene and play off one clan against another that the system eventually began to break down.

In the end it was the relative unity of a large grouping of clans favouring the deposed Stuart dynasty that led to the total destruction of the system when, after the Battle of Culloden in 1746, King George II, with ruthless

efficiency, destroyed the power of the chiefs for evermore and, in the process, destroyed much that was finest in Highland culture.

Today some chiefs, like Campbell of Argyll and MacLeod of MacLeod live in their ancestral castles; a few, like the former, live well because their forebears remained loyal to the Hanoverian dynasty and did not rise with Bonnie Prince Charlie in 1745; but they have no powers. Yet, throughout the world, large clan associations maintain the romance of the old tradition and there is still an indefinable sense of kinship among people of the same clan –

most emphatically among the emigré communities.

There are 84 chiefs on the Standing Council of Clan Chiefs which has mild, if not imaginary, discretion over the conduct of clan societies; they represent clans as varied as the Macdonalds of whom there are hundreds of thousands throughout the world, and the small Clan MacThomas, whose chief lives and works in London but visits the ancestral clan lands in Glenshee every August for a clan gathering.

A piper at Eilean Donan Castle, a former Mackenzie stronghold ▼

STRATHSPEY

MAP REF: 88NJ0222

Rising unobtrusively in the heights around the Corrieyairack Pass, the Spey is Scotland's second-longest river, almost 100 miles from source to sea. A minor public road follows it down to Laggan Bridge, and by the time it reaches Newtonmore it is ready to flow into the great valley between the Monadhliath and Cairngorm mountains. This is one of Scotland's busiest holiday areas, winter and summer.

Along this stretch of Strathspey, Newtonmore, Kingussie, Kincraig and Aviemore are all now bypassed by the A9 Perth-Inverness road.

Newtonmore is famous for two sports in particular. This was the first place in the Highlands where pony-trekking was organised; and Newtonmore shinty team, whose field is at the riverside park called the Eilan, is among the most successful in the Highlands. The Eilan is where Newtonmore Highland Games are held every August. They feature a rally of Macphersons – this is the heart of the Macpherson country, and the Clan Macpherson Museum, open on weekdays from May to September, is in the village.

By the riverside, Newtonmore also has a pleasant golf course. There is fishing, not just for salmon, brown trout and sea trout in the Spey and in the hill lochs nearby, but also for brown and rainbow trout at Loch Imrich, in the woods in the middle of the village itself.

Beyond Newtonmore is Kingussie, the capital of the district of Badenoch. The Highland Folk Museum, open from April to October, is in six acres of garden ground at the foot of Duke Street. There are indoor and outdoor displays, including a rebuilt Hebridean corn-mill. Footpaths lead into the birchwoods north of Kingussie, around the hillside golf course, designed by Harry Vardon.

Across the Spey is the ruin of Ruthven Barracks. Now preserved as an Ancient Monument, the barracks were extended from a 14th-century castle to act as a Government stronghold in Jacobite times. It was here, in 1746, that Prince Charles Edward Stuart announced to the remnants of the Jacobite army, ready to fight on after the defeat at Culloden, that the Rising was over.

Back on the north side of the Spey, before the village of Kincraig, but reached from the south by a turn off the A9 at Kingussie, is the Highland Wildlife Park. Open from March to the beginning of November, it was set up to gather together animals and birds which live in the Central Highlands today, and species like wolves and bison, lynx and bear, which have not lived in the wild in Scotland for centuries past. Some of the animals are in enclosures, but others roam free in a 200-acre parkland through which visitors may drive.

Kincraig itself is a smaller place than Kingussie, set among birches above the Spey and the waters of Loch Inch which, with the marshes alongside, are a world-famous wintering ground for whooper swans from the Arctic. From the Speybank walk there is a splendid view over Inshriach Forest to the Cairngorms.

Loch Inch is the base of a sailing and canoeing school, overlooked by the parish church on a hilltop site used for worship since the 7th century. Inside the church is an ancient Celtic church bell. Going beyond the loch, and turning either left or right on to the B970 from Ruthven Barracks, there is a choice of excellent walking country, even without going into the Cairngorms themselves.

Turning right on to B970 and then taking the minor road up the west side of Glen Feshie leads to a splendid Forestry Commission trail called the Rock Wood Ponds. Towards the end of the public road there is a forest picnic site at Tolvah, looking out over more open ground.

Turning left on to the B970 near Loch Inch leads to Feshiebridge, where there is another picnic site among the pines of Inshirach Forest. A minor road up the east side of Glen Feshie finishes at a nature trail at Achlean, at the very foot of the Cairngorms.

Continuing on the B970, past the alpine plant nursery at Inshriach House, another road to the right, about a mile and a half before the junction with the A951 at Inverdruie, goes to a car park and information centre at the Nature Conservancy Council's Loch an Eilein reserve. In the middle of the loch, on a rocky island, is the ruin of a 15th-century castle.

Back on the north side of the Spey, Aviemore is the main holiday resort in the district, built up in the late 1960s from a much more modest village. It has a fine array of hotels and chalets, an ice rink, a swimming pool, a shopping centre, fishing on rivers and lochs, a nature trail in the birchwoods immediately behind, and it provides the main accommodation for skiers on the Cairngorm slopes.

The route to the ski slopes is along the A851 past Inverdruie to Coylumbridge, then bearing right on to a road through the pine woods to Loch Morlich and the Glenmore Forest Park. At more than 1,000ft above sea level, Loch Morlich is used for sailing and canoeing, and even has a sandy beach; but it can be cold.

Beyond the loch at Glenmore there is a Forestry Commission information centre, the base for many enjoyable forest and hill walks. Scotland's only commercial reindeer herd is based nearby, and visitors can be taken to see them on their hill grazing. Farther into the glen there is the outdoor centre of Glenmore Lodge. Above the forest line, the 'ski road' swings up to car parks for the ski-tows and chairlifts to the upper slopes.

From Aviemore, the Spey can be followed by two different routes. The B970 reappears at Coylumbridge and heads along one side of the river towards the turn-off for Boat of Garten. As its name suggests, this village once had a chain-ferry across the Spey, where there is now a road bridge. It has a local museum and a fine golf course. And it is also the end of the volunteer-operated Strathspey Railway, which leaves the British Rail line at Aviemore and runs steam trains through the pine woods to Boat of Garten. There are plans to extend the line to Grantown-on-Spey.

After the Boat of Garten turn-off, the B970 heads for the village of Nethy Bridge. But a detour on minor roads, through the pines of Abernethy Forest, leads to the RSPB observation centre at the osprey nesting site on the north side of Loch Garten. The ospreys usually

LONG HIGHLAND TRAILS

There are two long-distance trails in the Highlands. The Speyside Way starts on Spey Bay, where there is a splendid profusion of birdlife and the Tugnet Icehouse (now a museum) which can be visited. The

Telford's famous bridge over the Spey ▼

◄ Balquhidder Church, where Rob Roy MacGregor is buried

STRATHYRE
MAP REF: 91NN5617

Strung along the A84 Callander-Lochearnhead road, Strathyre is a village hemmed in by steep hills and forest plantations. It is in the narrow valley of the River Balvag, which follows a short course from the foot of Loch Voil in Balquhidder, round a ninety-degree turn to the head of Loch Lubnaig, south of the village. When the now-dismantled Callander-Oban railway ran through here, Strathyre was an inland holiday resort, and it is still a centre for hill-walkers and anglers.

At the south end of the village there is a Forestry Commission information centre. A short forest trail goes up the hillside to the east. Across the valley, beyond the Balvag, a much stiffer climb leads to the summit of Ben Shian.

North-west of Strathyre, the valley of Balquhidder has a minor road along the north side of Loch Voil and Loch Doine. Rob Roy MacGregor is buried in the parish churchyard in Balquhidder village. Beyond Loch Doine, the public road ends at a picnic place at Inverlochlarig, near the site of Rob Roy's house, among the tangle of peaks and mountain passes which he exploited so well in his outlaw days.

STRONTIAN
MAP REF: 90NM8161

The crofting estate in the valley of the Strontian River is not owned by a private landlord, but by the government. Strontian village, beside the A861 Ardgour-Salen road, was rebuilt in the 1960s, and has a comprehensive information centre.

The minor road up the glen passes the nature trail through the Ariundle oakwood reserve, which leads towards disused lead mines on the open moorland above. These and other lead mines in the district were worked from 1722 to 1872. Strontium 90, a significant feature of nuclear fallout, takes its name from here.

The hill road, in sight of more old mines, some of which have recently been reopened to mine barytes, winds steeply over a pass to a Forestry Commission picnic site with views over Glenhurich Forest and the mountain ridges of Moidart, beyond Loch Shiel. It finishes at the isolated hamlet of Polloch, but the forestry road along the east side of Loch Shiel provides a spectacular walk to Glenfinnan.

---

arrive in the Highlands in April and leave for Africa in August.

Nethy Bridge is built around a Victorian hotel and the bridge over the River Nethy which gave it its name. Although it was once a timber and iron-working centre, it is now a quiet holiday resort.

From Nethy Bridge the B970 and then the A95 can be followed to Grantown-on-Spey, or a minor road can be taken, across the Spey and so to Grantown by a way of Dulnain Bridge. West of Dulnain Bridge, but still considered part of Strathspey in holiday terms, is Carrbridge. In the pine woods south of it is the Landmark Visitor Centre, with displays on the history and wildlife of Strathspey from the ice age to modern times and an exciting 'treetop trail'.

Grantown-on-Spey is the most elegant of the Strathspey resorts. It is basically still the planned town of 1766 laid out on the Grant family's estates.

There is an attractive golf course; there are famous fishing beats on the Spey, bowling, tennis and winter curling; the pine woods between town and river, and the hills that sweep up behind, provide some of the most beautiful walks in the Highlands. It is a good centre for climbing and skiing. And with all that, Grantown is a place where there is obviously no need to *rush*.

Way continues beside the Spey through Fochabers to reach the strange earth pillars at Aultdearg and then the attractive village of Craigellachie, with Telford's resplendent old bridge crossing the river.

From here the Way follows a disused railway line, from which there is a short spur to Dufftown, giving the opportunity to visit one of the Speyside distilleries. The main route continues to Aberlour, where the former station has a café and toilets, and on to Ballindalloch and Castle Grant.

The original proposal was for the Speyside Way to continue to Aviemore, but this has not proved possible, and instead it swings inland through the heather-covered hills to end at Tomintoul, the highest village in the Highlands.

The West Highland Way was Scotland's first long-distance footpath, opened in 1980. It runs for nearly 100 miles from Milngavie, north of Glasgow, to Fort William. The first section is through farmland and woods to Strathblane and then on to Balmaha on Loch Lomondside. The eastern shore of the famous loch is followed to Rowardennan and Inversnaid with its renowned falls.

A tough stretch follows to Glen Falloch, after which the walking becomes easier going to reach Crianlarich and through Glen Fillan to Tyndrum. Here the route swings north beside the railway and below steep Beinn Dorain to Bridge of Orchy and Victoria Bridge. From here the Way follows the old road over Blackmount to Glencoe – a superb 12-mile stretch with magnificent mountain views.

From Glencoe the Way climbs the Devil's Staircase, an old military road, to reach Kinlochleven before the final section through the Lairigmor pass to Glen Nevis.

THURSO

MAP REF: 85ND1168

The principal town of Caithness is at the centre of some of Scotland's finest coastal scenery. Westward, the A836 passes Dounreay, where the nuclear energy establishment can be visited, and the sands of Sandside and Melvich Bays, to the peninsula of Strathy Point. A walk along the private road leads to the dramatically sited lighthouse.

East of Thurso is Dunnet Bay, surely one of the finest and cleanest stretches of sandy beach on the British coastline. The area is noted for windsurfing, and championships have been held here in the past. A minor road leads to Dunnet Head, the most northerly point on the British mainland, where another lighthouse sits atop high cliffs, giving superb views over the Pentland Firth to Orkney.

Back in Thurso, the heritage museum in the Town Hall should be visited, and the attractive harbour area, where much restoration has taken place, has the ruined St Peter's Church at its heart. Ferries leave from Scrabster, two miles north of Thurso, for Stromness in Orkney.

South of the town, the flatter hinterland contains many lochs famed for their wild brown trout fishing. A vast roadless area, the Flow Country of dappled lochs and peatbogs, is crossed by the railway from Georgemas to Forsinard – a journey worth taking, for this is a landscape like no other in our islands. Sadly, there has been conflict here in recent years between conservation and forestry interests.

TOMINTOUL

MAP REF: 88NJ1618

At 1,160ft above sea level, Tomintoul is the highest village in the Highlands, at the northern end of

SKIING

From a means of getting around in hard winters in the early years of this century, skiing in Scotland has developed into an organised sport based at five centres. The main resort is on the northern side of the Cairngorms, where a ski road has been built from Aviemore to car parks at over 2,000ft in Coire Cas and Coire na Ciste.

The highest main road in Britain – the A93 from Perth to Braemar – also reaches over 2,000ft at its summit, where the Glenshee ski area is situated. This is the largest of Scotland's ski areas, with extensive runs on both sides of the road. There is also a ski centre at The Lecht, on the summit of the A939 road from Deeside to Tomintoul.

In the west, Glencoe has long been a favourite, particularly with experienced skiers. A car park off the A82 gives access to the lifts and tows on Meall a'Bhuiridh. Scotland's newest ski centre is at Aonach Mor, near Fort William, where a unique gondola run takes skiers – and many other visitors – to

▲ Skiers use an artificial slope to practice for the real thing

a restaurant at 2,200ft. From here lifts and tows ascend to nearly 4,000ft.

Skiing in Scotland has now settled into a regular pattern, with the main season running from Christmas to Easter. Newspapers and radio stations carry details of skiing conditions throughout the season and a telephone 'hotline' keeps up to date with the snowfalls – a commodity which has proved somewhat erratic in recent winters. Cross-country skiing is also popular, when conditions are right, with centres in the Glenmore Forest Park and in Glen Isla, and much informal activity elsewhere.

the dramatic Lecht Road which follows the military route of the 1750s between Deeside and Strathspey.

Despite its apparently isolated location among moorlands, farms and forests, Tomintoul is no casually laid-out place. It is to an exact pattern of streets, houses and extensive gardens approved by the Duke of Gordon, who let out parcels of land here in 1776.

The village square fits neatly into this pattern, with solidly built houses, shops and hotels, an information centre and a museum looking over the central green.

South of the village, and most conveniently reached on foot from it,

there is a three-mile country walk with fine views of the Avon valley. South-east along the A939 at the Well of the Lecht, a picnic site has been laid out beside a footpath to the site of an 18th-century ironstone mine.

Tomintoul is an angling centre. Trout and salmon permits can be bought in the village, for the fishing beats on the River Avon. The Avon rises high in the Cairngorms and winds down a long and lonely glen to pass west of Tomintoul, continuing south down Strath Avon, where the riverside B9136 is one of many pleasant roads in this often under-rated district.

TORRIDON

MAP REF: 86NG7563

While there will always be arguments about personal tastes in landscape, there is little doubt that the supreme example of mountain and sea-loch scenery on the mainland of Scotland is around Loch Torridon and Upper Loch Torridon in Wester Ross, with the subsidiary inlets of Loch Shieldaig and Loch Diabaig.

The major northern peaks – 3,232ft at Beinn Alligin, 2,995ft at Beinn

◀ Well of Lecht on the A939 from Tomintoul to Deeside, one of the highest roads in Britain

Dearg and right up to 3,456ft at the highest point of the seven summits of Liathach – have had 750 million years to mature. Torridonian sandstone is one of the oldest rocks in the world, and provides excellent mountaineering.

The entire area of Liathach and Beinn Alligin, together with the southern slopes of Beinn Dearg, are owned by the National Trust for Scotland, whose Torridon estate covers more than 16,000 acres.

From the south, the A896 from Lochcarron picks its way through Glen Shieldaig to reach tidal water at the head of Loch Shieldaig. A turning to the left is the start of the adventurous road round the northern tip of the Applecross peninsula, connecting previously remote villages like Ardheslaig and Kenmore, Arinacrinachd, Fearnbeg and Fearnmore.

Above Loch Shieldaig, the A896 skirts the attractively situated village of the same name, whose whitewashed houses look out to the pine woods of Shieldaig Island, another Trust property. Then it sweeps round the shoulder of a hill to follow a stunningly beautiful route above the south shore of Upper Loch Torridon.

From Shieldaig to Annat, the main road passes above the gorgeous rocky and wooded bays indenting the southern shore. But the near-at-hand view is only the foreground for the glorious mountain skyline across the loch.

Beyond the crofts of Annat, the A896 heads east up Glen Torridon and a minor road turns off left towards Inveralligin and Diabaig. Beside the junction is the Trust's Torridon visitor centre, open from June to September. A short distance

▲ Shieldaig is one of many attractive villages in Wester Ross

along the Diabaig road is the purpose-built Torridon youth hostel, a favourite with climbers and hill-walkers.

Torridon village looks to be precariously sited, below the great scree-slopes of Liathach. For a time, the road beyond it hugs the lochside, but then it turns sharply uphill above the pine woods of Torridon House to the bridge over the ravine of the Coire Mhic Nobuil burn. A car park at the bridge is the starting point for exhilarating walks on glen footpaths, which give the comparatively low-level explorer a fine view of the peaks, corries and pinnacles which are the playground of rock-climbers. The main path runs through the pines on the east bank of the burn, past waterfalls.

Now running high above the loch, with extensive views to the west and south, the Diabaig road comes to a junction where a side-turning to the left dips down to the spread-out lochside village of Inveralligin. It has a grassy parking space near the water's edge and striking views

across the loch to the end-on ridges of Beinn Shieldaig and Beinn Damh.

Back on the high road, past the turn-off to the crofting settlement of Wester Alligin, there is a steep, narrow and blind-cornered assault on the Bealach na Gaoithe – the Pass of the Wind. Over the pass, which has a viewpoint on the summit, the road plunges down to the scattered crofts and houses of Diabaig, on a gradient which reaches 1 in 3½ – the steepest public-road hill in Scotland.

The climb, however, is well worth the effort. Diabaig is set in a towering rocky amphitheatre round its own dramatic sea-loch. There is a car park by the pier, which is itself built up of multi-coloured rocks. Picnickers may have to fend off the attentions of the occasional well-mannered, but persistent, goat.

But perhaps Diabaig is best in the evening, when in the long, lingering West Highland dusk, the sun sets in a blaze of red and orange over Applecross, Rona and the northern peaks of Skye.

The glorious outline of Beinn Alligin mirrored in Loch Torridon ▼

THE TROSSACHS
MAP REF: 91NN5097

The popularity of the Trossachs, over the last 175 years, is due very largely to Sir Walter Scott. He first visited the district in 1790, and used it as the setting for both *The Lady of the Lake*, published in 1810, and for *Rob Roy*, which appeared eight years later. By 1820 the throngs of tourists were so great that the Duke of Montrose, on whose estates many of the places mentioned by Scott were located, had a cattle-drovers'

Ben Venue seen across Loch Venachar in the Trossachs ▼

track over the pass from Aberfoyle to Loch Achray rebuilt as a toll-road. The modern A821, opened as a public road only in 1931, uses that same route today.

This is an area of superb natural beauty. Most of it is remarkably unspoilt, thanks to the fact that nearly 70,000 acres are owned by two conservation-conscious organisations – the Forestry Commission and Strathclyde Regional Council Water Department. Both have opened up their 'empires' to provide a great variety of public access and recreation.

From the south, the main-road approach to the Trossachs is by the A81 from Glasgow. As it comes near to Aberfoyle, the A81 runs along the western edge of the flat, reclaimed land of Flanders Moss. The view ahead is totally different – a head-on collision with the Highland Line.

The diagonal ridge of the wooded and craggy Menteith Hills marks the north-east/south-west alignment of the Highland Boundary Fault. On the west side, this range of hills is covered with the spruce plantations

of Achray Forest, which stretches westwards across the Duke's Road to Ben Venue. Showing on a minor hilltop is a radio hut used by the fire-watching service of the Queen Elizabeth Forest Park, which extends from Achray to Loch Lomond. The lower-lying plantations south and west of Aberfoyle are in Loch Ard Forest.

The A81 itself does not go into Aberfoyle, but turns right along the southern edge of Achray Forest, past Aberfoyle's inevitably hilly golf course and the start of the Forestry Commission's Highland Edge Walk to the hilltop viewpoint of Lime Craig.

Where the A81 turns right, it is the A821 which goes left into the village of Aberfoyle. This is a tourist centre in a magnificent setting, starting at the banks of the infant River Forth and sweeping up the hillside at the first contour lines of the Highlands.

The Bailie Nicol Jarvie Hotel, at the road junction in the centre of the village, takes its name from one of the characters in *Rob Roy*. Immediately south of it, over an old

▲ The scene that Walter Scott made famous in 1810 with his epic poem *The Lady of the Lake*: the sharp little peak of Ben A'an above Loch Katrine, with Ellen's Isle clearly visible. A picture of matchless beauty indeed

Sunlight glitters on the waters of Loch Katrine; summer boat trips are understandably popular ▼

stone-arched bridge, is Kirkton of Aberfoyle, where the ruins of the original parish church recall another literary figure. The Reverend Robert Kirk, parish minister at the end of the 17th century, was an authority on the supernatural. He wrote a very detailed book called *The Secret Commonwealth of Elves, Fauns and Fairies* – and they were firmly believed in the district to have finally carried him away.

Beyond Kirkton, the public road ends near the manse where Sir Walter Scott stayed while writing about the district. Nearby is the start of the Doon Hill Fairy Trail, mainly for children, with the Reverend Robert Kirk's story in mind.

West of Aberfoyle, the B829 goes along the foot of steep oak-covered hills to Milton, where there is another forest walk, alongside the tree-fringed Loch Ard with its distant view of Ben Lomond, then on to a junction for Stronachlachar on Loch Katrine and down to Loch Lomondside at Inversnaid.

The most spectacular drive in the Trossachs, and for miles around, is on the A821 as it begins its steep and sharp-cornered climb north from Aberfoyle – the Duke's Road. Off to the right, above the village, is the David Marshall Lodge, a grand viewpoint and the visitor centre for the Queen Elizabeth Forest Park.

Probably the wildest part of the landscape around the Duke's Road is at the old Aberfoyle slate quarries, worked for more than 200 years till 1958. The quarry road survives. Among the deserted workings and spoil heaps there are traces of the quarry village, the smithy, the powder magazine, the mineral railway and the horse tramway which took the finished slates towards the main railway line – also a thing of the past – at Aberfoyle.

Before the top of the Duke's Road, a turning to the right leads into the Achray Forest Drive. Open daily from Easter to September, its seven miles of gravel road pass three lochs, a dozen parking places, information points, a children's play area, viewpoints and picnic sites at places named after the local tree cover, like Larch Point, Pine Ridge and Spruce Glen.

As it comes down off the hills again, the A821 runs along the woodland fringe at the west end of Loch Achray, where there is another parking and picnic area. The loch is used for sailing, water-skiing and angling. On the north side, after the main road turns right at a T-junction, there is a car park near the start of the footpath to the top of Ben A'an. Although the summit is no higher than 1,520ft, it is an exposed and genuine peak.

From the junction at the west end of Loch Achray, another road turns left through a little pass to Trossachs Pier in a wooded bay near the foot of Loch Katrine. This is the start of the Water Department estate, which includes the entire catchment area of the loch.

There is plenty of car parking space at Trossachs Pier, beside a tea-room and a fascinating visitor centre, open from May to September, which explains about the work of the department, about its fish hatchery, forest plantations, sawmill, sheep and cattle farms. The landward parts of the estate work for their living, too.

Although the public road ends at Trossachs Pier, there are two ways of reaching Stronachlachar at the far end of the loch – and they can be combined, one out and one back. The first is to walk or cycle along the tarmac service road along the north shore, past Glengyle, the birthplace of Rob Roy MacGregor. The other is to sail the eight miles on the department's beautiful Victorian steamer *Sir Walter Scott*, which makes the run from May to September. If its red and white awnings are very turn-of-the-century, it has the modern feature, in a pollution-conscious era, of burning smokeless fuel.

Back at Loch Achray, the A821 continues along the north shore of Loch Venachar to join the A84 at Kilmahog. A right turn leads to Callander, the town which is the eastern gateway to the Trossachs. It has hotels, boarding houses, shops and tucked-away caravan sites. Permits can be bought for loch and river fishing, and there is an attractive golf course backed by peaceful beech woods.

THE JACOBITE RISINGS.

Not all Highlanders were Jacobites, and not all Jacobites were Highlanders – or even Scots. There was a larger interest. The political goal of the Jacobites between 1689 and 1746 was the restoration to the throne of the United Kingdom of the Royal House of Stuart.

Last of the direct line of Stuart kings was James VII of Scotland and II of England, deposed in the Glorious Revolution of 1688. He gave the movement its name – *Jacobus* is the Latin version of James. The Risings of 1708, 1715, 1719 and 1745 were in favour of his exiled son, who was also called James.

But the most charismatic character in the Jacobite story was *his* son Charles Edward Stuart, Bonnie Prince Charlie. That Christian name was no casual diminutive. It is simply the English form of the Gaelic *Tearlaich* or Charles. The defeat of his army at

Culloden in 1746 consigned the Stuarts from then on to the footnotes of history.

All the Jacobite Risings were failures in the end. They were mostly financed by France and

▲ Jacobite heroine Flora Macdonald

Spain, making mischief on the greater European scene. But there is still a strong attachment, in many parts of the Highlands, to the memory of those Jacobite days and the romantic figure of Bonnie Prince Charlie, the Young Chevalier.

ULLAPOOL

MAP REF: 84NH1294

Approached by the A835 along the shore of Loch Broom, Ullapool is first seen from the brow of a hill. It is an attractive and unexpectedly sizeable village with a frontage of whitewashed houses and hotels, arranged in regular style on a curve of land which guards its harbour from the open sea. The location and layout were settled by the British Fisheries Society, which founded Ullapool in 1788 as a base for the rich herring fishing of the Minch.

Ullapool is still an important port. It is the mainland terminal of the car-ferry to Stornoway on the Island of Lewis. And Loch Broom is still busy with fishing boats, whose

catches are often bought by foreign factory ships anchored offshore.

However, Ullapool is also a holiday resort. It is a good sailing centre, and there is another one at Altna h-Airbhe on the wild peninsula on the far side of the loch, reached by a weekday ferry which runs from May until September. That ferry link makes it possible to walk over the peninsula to Dundonnell and to Scoraig on Little Loch Broom. Dundonnell House gardens are occasionally open during the summer. And Scoraig is that rarity in modern times, a flourishing village which has no road connection with the rest of mainland Scotland – and

The harbour front at Ullapool, a planned 18th-century town ▼

has, indeed, turned down the chance of having one built.

Boat-hirers at Ullapool run cruises to the scattered Summer Isles, home of seals and seabirds. Loch Broom is a noted sea-angling centre. There is also trout and salmon fishing close by, in the River Ullapool and Loch Achall from which it flows.

One of the original buildings set up by the British Fisheries Society has been turned into a museum. It was once a fish-curing house, and even now the salt is said to seep from the roof-beams.

WESTER ROSS

MAP REF: 86NG8076

Mountains and seascapes dominate this superb area, where there is plenty of space and the possibilities for recreation are endless.

Heading north from Gairloch, the A832 soon reaches Poolewe and, a mile farther on, the famous Inverewe Gardens, created from a bare, windswept site by Osgood Mackenzie in the 19th century and now in the care of the National Trust for Scotland. Here you will find rare plants and trees from all over the world.

The road continues, with fine views both out to sea and inland, to Aultbea and then to Laide on Gruinard Bay. Turning left here leads to Mellon Udrigle, where the sandy beach has a most spectacular view northwards to the mountains of Sutherland and south to the mighty peaks of An Teallach. From Achgarve, a rough road can be walked across the peninsula to the deserted village of Slaggan, above another fine sandy beach. It has a very special atmosphere.

The road continues round Gruinard Bay, whose island was used for germ warfare experiments in World War II but has now been decontaminated, and reaches Little Loch Broom. From Dundonnell you can walk up to Loch Toll an Lochain, dramatically sited below An Teallach, and a side road leads to Badrallach and the walk to Scoraig. This is one of the few communities in Britain with no road access – by choice! The people here run their own school and have chosen their remote way of life for its particular quality.

The road continues over high moorland, passing a viewpoint with a magnificent view down Loch Broom, to join the A835 at Braemore Junction. There are car parks on both roads giving access to the Corrieshalloch Gorge, a dramatic box canyon (NTS) containing the 150ft Falls of Measach, viewed from a small suspension bridge. It is

▲ Looking across Loch Ewe from the famous gardens at Inverewe, founded by Osgood Mackenzie and now in the care of the National Trust for Scotland

museum in Bank Row has an award-winning exhibition on herring fishing, and a more modern industry can be seen at Caithness Glass, on Harrowhill.

North of Wick, past the airfield, are the twin ruins of castles Sinclair and Girnigoe, precariously perched on the clifftop. One-time strongholds of the Earls of Caithness, they look north along the long sweep of Sinclairs Bay, its beaches swept by North Sea rollers. The A9 continues north to John o' Groats, passing Auckengill, where the John Nicolson Museum tells the story of the mysterious brochs and has a 4,000-year-old beaker as a prized exhibit.

▲ A barometer on the harbour front at Wick is an aid to seamen

intriguing to note that the bridge was designed by Sir John Fowler, better known for his work on a rather larger construction, the Forth Rail Bridge!

The A835 runs alongside Loch Broom to Ullapool, passing Lael with its forest garden and walks. North of Ullapool, the road passes the sailing and sea-angling centre at Ardmair to Drumrunie and Knockan Cliff, where there is a visitor centre for the vast Inverpolly National Nature Reserve. Walks enable the visitor to appreciate the special nature of the geology here, and there are fine views of the Coigach peaks.

A minor road from Drumrunie passes Loch Lurgainn, which can be fished and is also the start point for the walk up Stac Pollaidh with its fantastic collection of rock towers and pinnacles. At the far end of Loch Bad a Ghaill, a narrow and twisting road follows the western edge of the Inverpolly reserve to Inverkirkaig and Lochinver. Straight on at Badnagyle leads you to Achiltibuie, the main village in Coigach, strung out along the roadside looking out over Badentarbat Bay to the Summer Isles.

There is sea-angling here, boat trips to the islands, and good hotels. A special attraction is the Hydroponicum where, in this wild Highland setting, you will find the 'garden of the future' – propagation without soil. Strawberries, figs, bananas, vines and vegetables grow

in profusion here under a glass dome. There are four 90-minute tours daily from April to early October.

You can also visit the Smokehouse, on the road from Achiltibuie to Reiff, to see how fish and game are smoked, and sample the delicious results, perhaps enjoying a matchless Wester Ross sunset and pondering your choice of walk for the following day as you do so.

WICK
MAP REF: 85ND3650

Wick, a Norse name simply meaning a bay, is the old centre of Caithness. In the town itself, the heritage

South of Wick, the exposed coastline is indented by 'geos', deep gashes cut by the action of the sea. At Whaligoe, an extraordinary flight of over 300 steps leads down to a tiny harbour at the foot of the cliff. Signs of more ancient civilisations abound, including the mysterious Hill o' Many Stanes at Clyth, its purpose still unknown to us, and the Grey Cairns of Camster, on a minor road reached from near Lybster.

The road can be followed to Watten, where a right turn leads on to the A882 past the site of the Battle of Altimarlach (1680) and so back to Wick.

The gaunt ruins of the twin castles of Sinclair and Girnigoe, just north of Wick, sit on the very edge of the cliff ▼

◀ Branklyn Gardens, Perth (NTS)

PLACES TO VISIT

This is just a selection of the numerous places to visit in the Scottish Highlands. For a fuller list, contact the Scottish Tourist Board (see page 000).

The abbreviations HS and NTS stand for properties in the care of Historic Scotland and the National Trust for Scotland respectively.

BH = bank holiday
Etr = Easter

ABERDEEN

Art Gallery, Schoolhill. *Collection of 18th- to 20th-century art.* Open all year, daily.

Jonah's Journey, Rosemount Pl. *Aspects of life in Biblical times: children can dress up, spin, weave etc.* Open all year, Mon to Fri, plus weekends by arrangement.

Maritime Museum, Provost Ross's House, Shiprow. *Models, paintings and audio-visual displays tell the story of Aberdeen's shipbuilding and fishing industries.* Open all year, Mon to Sat.

Satrosphere, The Discovery Place, Justice Mill Lane. *Hands-on science and technology centre.* Open all year, daily except Tue.

Storybook Glen, Maryculter, 5m SW of Aberdeen. *Children's fantasy land brought to life.* Open Mar to Oct, daily; Nov to Feb, weekends only.

ACHILTIBUIE

The Hydroponicum. *Space-age gardening without soil. Crops include bananas, figs and vines.* Open Apr to Oct, daily.

ACHNACARRY

Clan Cameron Museum, 15m NW of Fort William. Clan and Jacobite memorabilia in reconstructed 17th-century croft house. Open Etr to Oct, daily.

ALFORD

Alford Valley Railway, Murray Park. *Narrow-gauge passenger railway: steam at weekends. Exhibitions.* Open Apr, May and Sep weekends; Jun to Aug daily.

Craigievar Castle (NTS), 6m S of Alford. *Fairytale castle dating from 1610.* Castle open May to Sep, daily; grounds open all year.

Grampian Transport Museum. *Collection of vintage road and rail vehicles.* Open Apr to Sep, daily.

FACT FILE
CONTENTS

▲ Craigievar Castle, near Alford (NTS)

Kildrummy Castle (HS), 10m W of Alford. *Impressive ruins of 13th-century stronghold.* Open Apr to Sep daily; Oct to Mar weekends only.

Kildrummy Castle Gardens, 10m W of Alford. *Alpine garden in an old quarry, water gardens and woods.* Open Apr to Oct, daily.

ARMADALE, ISLE OF SKYE

Clan Donald Centre. *Award-winning centre with Museum of the Isles and 40-acre garden.* Open Apr to Oct, daily. Gardens open all year.

AVIEMORE

Loch Garten, 8m NE of Aviemore. *RSPB centre with viewing of osprey nest.* Open Apr to Aug, daily.

Rothiemurchus Estate Visitor Centre, 1m E of Aviemore. *Wildlife and craft displays, whisky centre, estate tours.* All year, daily.

Strathspey Railway. *Steam trains to Boat of Garten.* Jun to Sep, daily. Apr, May, Oct weekends.

BALLATER

Balmoral Castle, 8m W of Ballater. *Scottish home of Royal Family.* Grounds and ballroom open May to Jul, Mon to Sat.

Corgarff Castle (HS), 15m NW of Ballater. *Sixteenth-century tower house in dramatic situation.* Open all year, daily.

Royal Lochnagar Distillery, 6m W of Ballater. *Tours and tastings.* Open Etr to Oct, daily. Nov to Etr, Mon to Fri.

BANCHORY

Crathes Castle (NTS), 3m E of Banchory. *Magnificent interior and superb gardens.* Castle open Apr to Oct, daily; grounds all year, daily.

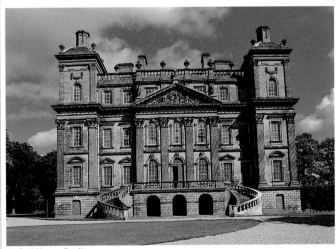

▲ Duff House, Banff

BANFF

Duff House (HS), ½m S of Banff. *Fine Georgian baroque mansion by William Adam.* Open Apr to Sep, daily.

North-East Falconry Centre, 4m S of Banff. *Flying displays of owls, hawks and falcons.* Open all year daily.

BETTYHILL

Strathnaver Museum, Farr. *Highland Clearances displays and domestic items in former church.* Open Apr to Oct, Mon to Sat.

BLAIR ATHOLL

Atholl Country Collection. *Displays of local life and history.* Open May to Oct, daily.

Blair Castle. *Home of the Duke of Atholl: 31 rooms filled with treasures. Gardens and deer park.* Open Apr to Oct, daily.

BRAEMAR

Braemar Castle, 1m E of Braemar. *Turreted stronghold with many interesting relics.* Open May to early Oct, daily.

BUCKIE

Buckie Museum and Peter Anson Gallery. *Maritime museum including displays on navigation and coopering.* Open all year, Mon to Sat.

COMRIE

Scottish Tartans Museum. *All aspects of tartans from a dye garden to costumes.* Open Apr to Oct, daily; Nov to Mar, check times locally.

CRIEFF

Glenturret Distillery, 1m W of Crieff. *Scotland's oldest distillery. Tours and tastings.* Open Mar to Dec, Mon to Fri; Apr to Oct, Sat also.

Innerpeffray Library, 4½m SE of Crieff. *Scotland's oldest free lending library (1691) with bibles and other rare books.* Open all year, daily except Thu.

CROMARTY

Hugh Miller's Cottage (NTS), Church St. *Thatched cottage with displays on the life of the eminent geologist.* Open Apr to Sep, daily.

DORNIE

Eilean Donan Castle. *Restored castle on islet in Loch Duich.* Open Etr to Sep, daily.

DOUNREAY

AEA Nuclear Research Station. *Exhibits relating to fast reactors and nuclear energy.* Open Etr to Sep, daily.

DRUMNADROCHIT

Loch Ness Lodge Visitor Centre. *Large-screen cinema films on the loch and the monster, plus local history.* Open all year, daily.

Official Loch Ness Monster Exhibition. *Multi-media presentation covering the story of the fabled monster.* Open Apr to Oct, daily. Nov to Mar, check times locally.

Urquhart Castle (HS), 2m S of Drumnadrochit. *Favourite 'monster watching' spot on the banks of Loch Ness.* Open all year, daily.

DUFFTOWN

Balvenie Castle (HS), 1m N of Dufftown. *Picturesque ruins next to Glenfiddich distillery.* Open Apr to Sep daily.

Glenfiddich Distillery. *Visitor centre, tours and tastings.* Open all year, Mon to Fri, plus weekends Etr to Sep.

DUNBEATH

Lhaidhay Croft Museum, 1m N of Dunbeath. *Thatched Caithness longhouse and other old buildings.* Open Etr to Sep, daily.

DUNKELD

Dunkeld Cathedral (HS). *Twelfth- and 15th-century church in superb setting.* Open all year, daily.

Little Houses (NTS). *Two rows of restored 17th-century cottages (view from outside only).* Visitor centre in The Square open Apr to Dec, Mon to Sat plus Sun Jun to Aug.

DURNESS

Smoo Cave, 1m E of Durness. *Vast caves in limestone cliff. Boat trips.* Open all year, daily (check access with Durness tourist office).

◀ Loch Ness Exhibition, Drumnadrochit

ELGIN

Elgin Cathedral (HS). *Substantial ruins with fine octagonal chapter house.* Open Apr to Oct, daily; Nov to Mar, daily except Thu.

Elgin Museum, 1 High St. *Includes famous fossil collection.* Open Apr to Sep, Tue to Sat.

Pluscarden Abbey, 6m SW of Elgin. *Occupied by an active Benedictine community. Special events and exhibitions.* Open all year, daily.

FETTERCAIRN

Fasque House, ½m N of Fettercairn. *Home of the Gladstone family since 1829. Displays including servants quarters, gardens and deer park.* Open May to Sep, daily except Wed.

FOCHABERS

Baxter's of Fochabers, 1m W of Fochabers. *Visitor centre, factory tours, Victorian kitchen.* Open Mar to Dec, Mon to Fri; May to Sep weekends also.

Folk Museum, High St. *Converted church with large collection of old horse-drawn vehicles and fascinating displays of local life.* Open all year, daily.

Tugnet Ice House, 5m N of Fochabers. *Exhibitions on salmon fishing, geography and wildlife.* Open Jun to Sep, daily.

FORRES

Brodie Castle (NTS), 4½m W of Forres. *Handsome gabled castle with extensive grounds.* Open Etr to Sep, daily, plus weekends in Oct.

FORT WILLIAM

West Highland Museum. *Displays on Highland life and history.* Open all year, Mon to Sat.

GAIRLOCH

Gairloch Heritage Museum. *Award-winning displays of local life and history.* Open Etr to Sep, Mon to Sat.

Inverewe Garden (NTS), 6m NE of Gairloch. *Rare and sub-tropical plants and trees from all over the world. Garden open all year, daily; visitor centre open Apr to Oct, daily.*

GLAMIS

Angus Folk Museum (NTS). *Extensive collection of domestic and agricultural bygones.* Open Apr to Sep, daily.

Glamis Castle. *Well-known former Royal Family home with much to see.* Open mid-Apr to mid-Oct, daily.

GLENCOE

Glencoe and North Lorn Folk Museum, Glencoe village. *Thatched cottages with local exhibits.* Open May to Sep, Mon to Sat.

Glencoe Visitor Centre (NTS), 3m N of Glencoe village. *Displays on wildlife and history of the area.* Open Apr to Oct, daily.

GOLSPIE

Dunrobin Castle, 2m N of Golspie. *Home of the Duke of Sutherland. Magnificent building and formal gardens.* Open May, Mon to Thu; Jun to Sep, daily.

Dunrobin Castle, just north of Golspie, is open to view in summer ▼

GRANTOWN-ON-SPEY

Speyside Heather Centre, 4m SW of Grantown. *Gardens with over 300 heathers, exhibition on traditional uses of the plant, craft shop.* Open Mar to Oct, daily; Nov, Dec, Feb, Mon to Sat. Closed Jan.

HELMSDALE

Timespan. *Award-winning exhibition of Highland history and culture.* Open Apr to Oct, daily.

HUNTLY

Huntly Castle (HS). *Impressive ruins with notable heraldic decorations.* Open all year, daily; closed Fri in winter.

INVERNESS

Castle Stuart, 5m E of Inverness. *Jacobean furnishings and historic relics.* Open May to Sep, daily.

Culloden Battlefield (NTS), 4m E of Inverness. *Site of the last battle on British soil in 1746. Audio-visual display, clan graves, etc.* Centre open Mar to Dec, daily; site always open.

Highland Wineries, Moniack Castle, 7m W of Inverness. *Wine-making centre, tours and tastings.* Open all year, Mon to Sat.

Museum and Art Gallery, Castle Wynd. *Local history, Jacobite relics, piping memorabilia.* Open all year, Mon to Sat, plus Sun in Jul and Aug.

KEMNAY

Castle Fraser (NTS), 3m S of Kemnay. *The largest and grandest of the Castles of Mar.* Castle open May to Sep, daily; plus weekends in Oct. Grounds open all year, daily.

KINCRAIG

Highland Wildlife Park. *Native species in natural settings – wolves, wildcats etc.* Open Apr to Oct, daily.

KINGUSSIE

Highland Folk Museum. *Crafts, mill, black house.* Open Apr to Oct, daily; Nov to Mar, Mon to Fri.

Ruthven Barracks (HS), 1m SE of Kingussie. *Remains of infantry barracks blown up by retreating Jacobites in 1746.* Open all year, daily.

KINLOCHEWE

Beinn Eighe National Nature Reserve. *Visitor centre, 2m N of Kinlochewe, open May to Sep, daily; woodland and mountain trails open all year. A guide leaflet is available.*

▲ Cawdor Castle, associated with Macbeth, dates from 1372 and has much to attract the visitor, including beautiful grounds

KIRRIEMUIR

Barrie's Birthplace (NTS), Brechin Rd. *Exhibition of the life and work of the author of Peter Pan.* Etr plus May to Sep, daily.

LOCH AWE

Cruachan Power Station, 20m E of Oban. *Exhibition plus bus trips to turbine room deep inside the mountain.* Open Etr to Oct, daily.

MINTLAW

Agricultural Heritage Centre, Aden Country Park, 1m W of Mintlaw. *Two centuries of farming history excitingly illustrated.* Open May to Sep, daily; Apr and Oct, weekends only.

MONTROSE

House of Dun (NTS), 4m W of Montrose. *Palladian house by Adam, recently restored.* Open mid-Apr to mid-Oct, daily.

NAIRN

Cawdor Castle, 5m SW of Nairn. *A drawbridge, well, putting green and trails are among the attractions.* Open May to Sep, daily.

Fort George (HS), 5m W of Nairn. *Impressive 18th-century stronghold.* Fort open all year, daily. Museum open Apr to Sep, daily; Oct to Mar, Mon to Fri.

OBAN

Dunstaffnage Castle (HS), 3m N of Oban. *Well preserved 13th-century castle.* Open Apr to Sep, daily; Oct to Mar, closed Thu pm and Fri.

Oban Glass, Lochavullin Estate. *Paperweights made and sold.* Shop open all year, Mon to Fri plus Sat am in summer. Factory viewing all year, Mon to Fri.

Sea Life Centre, 10m N of Oban. *Unique displays of marine life from eels to seals with 'touch tank' for children.* Open Mar to Nov, daily.

PERTH

Branklyn Garden (NTS), Dundee Rd. *Two acres with outstanding rhododendrons.* Open Mar to Oct, daily.

Caithness Glass, Inveralmond, 2m N of Perth. *Watch paperweights being made, plus museum and shop.* Open all year, daily.

Huntingtower Castle (HS), 2m W of Perth. *Castellated mansion with fine painted ceilings.* Open all year, daily.

Perth Museum and Art Gallery, George St. *Fine and applied art, local and natural history.* Open all year, Mon to Sat.

Scone Palace, 3m N of Perth. *Superb porcelain, furniture, clocks etc, plus extensive grounds with walks and adventure playground.* Open Etr to Oct, daily.

▲ Small boats line up across the harbour at Mallaig

permit vary tremendously, ranging from £1 per day to upwards of £2,000 per week. Permits can be obtained from local post offices, shops and hotels, and many of the tourist area boards (see page 77–8) publish their own guides giving contact addresses, local clubs and permit details.

▲ Superb angling country

PETERCULTER

Drum Castle (NTS), 3m W of Peterculter. *Thirteenth-century tower with fine mansion attached.* Open May to Sep, daily; Oct weekends only.

PETERHEAD

Arbuthnot Museum and Art Gallery, St Peter St. *Includes Arctic and whaling displays.* Open all year, Mon to Sat.

PITLOCHRY

Edradour Distillery, 2m E of Pitlochry. *Scotland's smallest, and virtually unchanged since built.* Open Mar to Oct, daily; Nov to Feb, Sat only.

Power Station and Dam. *Visitor centre, viewing gallery and fish pass for salmon run.* Open Apr to Oct, daily.

PITMEDDEN

Haddo House (NTS), 4m N of Pitmedden. *Adam mansion with country park.* House open Apr to Oct, daily; park open all year, daily.

Pitmedden Garden (NTS). *Seventeenth-century garden with museum of farming life.* Open May to Sep, daily.

RHYNIE

Leith Hall (NTS), 3½m NE of Rhynie. *Jacobite relics in house, lovely gardens.* House open May to Sep, daily; Oct, weekends only. Grounds open all year, daily.

ROSEMARKIE

Groam House Museum. *Symbol stone and other Pictish relics, video programme.* Open May to Sep, daily.

STONEHAVEN

Dunnottar Castle (HS), 1½m S of Stonehaven. *Spectacular promontory site.* Open Apr to Oct, daily; Nov to Mar, Mon to Fri.

Stonehaven Tolbooth Museum, Old Pier. *Former storehouse and prison, now a fishing and local history museum.* Open Jun to Sep, daily except Tue.

TOMATIN

Tomatin Distillery. *Tours and tastings.* Open May to Sep, Mon to Fri.

TOMINTOUL

Tomintoul Museum, The Square. *Folklore, natural history and geology.* Open Apr to Sep, daily.

TURRIFF

Fyvie Castle (NTS), 8m SE of Fyvie. *Grand example of Scottish baronial architecture with sumptuous interior.* Castle open Apr to Sep, daily; Oct, weekends only. Grounds open all year, daily.

WICK

Caithness Glass, Harrowhill. *All aspects of glassmaking on view.* Factory tours all year, Mon to Fri; shop open all year, Mon to Sat.

Wick Heritage Centre, Bank Row. *Prize-winning exhibition of the herring fishing industry.* Open Jun to Sep, Mon to Sat.

SPORTS AND ACTIVITIES

The following activities are among those Scotland is best known for. Many hotels offer special interest holidays of all kinds, and information about these can be obtained from the Scottish Tourist Board.

ANGLING

Scotland offers the angler a wide choice of both river and loch fishing, where salmon and brown, sea, and rainbow trout are to be found.
  The fishing season varies according to the individual river or loch, as well as with the species. Prices of

CYCLING

Apart from a network of quiet roads, ideal for cycling, Scotland has an increasing number of designated routes for cyclists only. In several cases these follow former railway lines and Forestry Commission access roads. Further information about these routes is available from local tourist information centres.

The following is a selection of establishments in the Highlands that hire out bicycles.

Aberdeen, *Aberdeen Cycle Centre,* 188 King St (0224 644542).

Aviemore, *Ellis Brigham,* 9/10 Grampian Rd (0479 810175).

Crieff, *Green Bicycle Co* (0764 2080).

Fort William, *Off-beat Bikes,* 4 Inverlochy Place (0397 2663).

Inverness, *Highland Cycles,* 26 Greig St (0463 710462).

Ullapool, *Ullapool Mountain Bike Hire,* 11 Pulteney St (0854 2260).

For a more comprehensive list contact tourist information centres.

GOLF

This is one of the premier sporting activities in Scotland and there are over 400 courses throughout the country.
  Round and day tickets are available at most courses, and some offer

weekly tickets.

A Golf Map which details Scotland's courses and includes contact addresses and telephone numbers is available from the Scottish Tourist Board.

SKIING

There are five ski resorts in the Scottish Highlands, all catering for mixed abilities. They are located at Aonach Mor and Glencoe near Fort William, Aviemore, and Glenshee and The Lecht in the Grampian Mountains.

Cross-country skiing is also available at Glenisla, Glenmore Forest and Glenmulliach.

Ski schools and equipment are available at all the resorts.

For further details send for the Ski Scotland brochure published by the Scottish Tourist Board.

▲ Made it! Group photo on the summit of Cairn Gorm

WALKING

The Scottish Highlands provide the visitor with wonderful walking country, ranging from rugged mountainous areas to gentle lowland. *Walks and Trails in Scotland*, published by the Scottish Tourist Board, gives details of nearly 200 walks of all kinds. Contact the Forestry Commission (page 77) for their selection of forest walks and trails, or the area tourist boards for local information.

Don't forget that hill walking can be hazardous, and Scottish mountains are subject to rapid changes in the weather. Proper clothing and equipment are essential when taking to the hills, and always leave word as to your whereabouts.

It is also very important to remember that the stalking and shooting season occurs between August and October, so when walking during that period always check with the local estates or farmers that your intended route will not interfere with these activities. Tourist information centres can also give advice about this.

USEFUL INFORMATION

ADDRESSES

Edinburgh and Scottish Travel Centre, Waverley Market, 3 Princes Street, Edinburgh EH2 2QP (031 557 1700).
This office provides an information service covering all aspects of holidaying in Scotland, and includes free literature.

Ferry Services
Caledonian MacBrayne, The Pier, Gourock (0475 33755).

Western Ferries, 16 Woodside Crescent, Glasgow (041 3329766).

P&O Ferries, Orkney & Shetland Services, Jamieson's Quay, Aberdeen (0224 572615).

Forestry Commission,
231 Corstorphine Road, Edinburgh EH12 7AT (031 334 0303).

Historic Scotland (HS), 20 Brandon Street, Edinburgh EH3 5RA (031 244 3101).
Historic Scotland is a Government agency which preserves and maintains a major part of Scotland's heritage of buildings.

National Trust for Scotland (NTS), 5 Charlotte Square, Edinburgh EH2 4DU (031 226 5922).

Scottish Tourist Board (main office), 23 Ravelston Terrace, Edinburgh EH4 3EU (031 332 2433).

Scottish Youth Hostels Association, 7 Glebe Crescent, Stirling FK8 2JA (0786 51181).

AREA TOURIST BOARDS

These offices provide information for the traveller through their tourist information centres. A full list of these centres is obtainable from the Scottish Tourist Board main office (see above). For full information on a particular area, write to, or telephone, the appropriate office below.

Aberdeen ·
City of Aberdeen Tourist Board, St Nicholas House, Broad Street, Aberdeen AB9 1DE (0224 632727).
Gordon District Tourist Board, as above.

Arbroath
Angus Tourist Board, Market Place, Arbroath, Tayside DD11 1HR (0241 72609/76680).

Aviemore
Aviemore and Spey Valley Tourist Board, Grampian Road, Aviemore, Highland PH22 1PP (0479 810363).

Banchory
Kincardine and Deeside Tourist Board, 45 Station Road, Banchory, Grampian AB3 3XX (03302 2066).

Banff
Banff and Buchan Tourist Board, Collie Lodge, Banff AB4 1AU (02612 2419).

Dornoch
Sutherland Tourist Board, The Square, Dornoch, Highland IV25 3SD (0862 810400).

Elgin
Tourist Information Centre, 17 High Street, Elgin, Grampian IV30 1EG (0343 542666).

Fort William
Fort William and Lochaber Tourist Board, Cameron Centre, Cameron Square, Fort William, Highland PH33 6AJ (0397 703781).

Inverness
Inverness, Loch Ness and Nairn Tourist Board, 23 Church Street, Inverness IV1 1EZ (0463 234353).

Ross and Cromarty Tourist Board, Information Centre, North Kessock, Inverness IV1 1XB (046373 505).

Perth
Perthshire Tourist Board, 45 High Street, Perth PH1 5TJ (0738 38353).

Portree
Isle of Skye and South West Ross Tourist Board, Portree, Isle of Skye (0478 2137).

Wick
Caithness Tourist Board, Whitechapel Road, Wick, Highland KW1 4EA (0955 2596).

NATIONAL TOURIST ROUTES
Signs consisting of white lettering on a brown background indicate National Tourist Routes. These pick out some of the most outstanding scenery and interesting places in Scotland.

THEMED TRAILS
There are also a number of car trails in the Scottish Highlands based on a single theme. For example, a trail in Speyside takes in eight malt whisky distilleries. Tourist information centres can supply literature about these trails and other touring routes in the area.

THEATRES AND CINEMAS
There are theatres at Aberdeen, Arbroath, Biggar, Braemar, Dervaig, Dundee, Inverness, Perth, Pitlochry, St Andrews, Tarves, Thurso, and cinemas at Aberdeen, Arbroath, Blairgowrie, Buckle, Campbeltown, Cupar, Dundee, Elgin, Fort William, Inverness, Inverurie, Montrose, Perth, Peterhead and St Andrews.

CUSTOMS AND EVENTS
Apart from those listed here, numerous arts festivals and Highland gatherings take place throughout the summer. Contact the area tourist boards for more details of local events.

JANUARY
Burning the Clavie
Burghead (11th). *Half a whisky barrel is lit and paraded round the village and left at Doonie Hill.*

EASTER
Inverness Folk Festival
Inverness (Easter Weekend). *Various musical events in the town.*

MAY
Atholl Highlanders Parade
Blair Castle, Blair Atholl (last Saturday). *Parade of this private army, the only one in Britain.*

Perth Festival of the Arts
Perth (end of the month). *Drama, music and the arts.*

JUNE
Riding the Marches
Aberdeen (part of the Bon Accord Festival held in mid-June). *A procession walks the city's boundaries over two days.*

Maggie Fair
Garmouth (4th Saturday). *Fair named after Lady Margaret Ker, with King Charles II connections – stalls, sideshows, teas.*

JULY
Caithness Highland Gathering and Games
Thurso (early in the month). *Traditional Highland sports.*

AUGUST
Glenfinnan Highland Games.
Tossing the caber, piping, Highland dancing, etc.

These are just two of over 60 similar events held in the Highlands during the summer months.

SEPTEMBER
Ben Nevis Hill Race
Fort William (1st Saturday). *Gruelling scramble up Ben Nevis.*

Braemar Gathering
Braemar (1st Saturday). *Massed pipe bands and Highland games with royalty usually in attendance.*

DECEMBER
Fireballs Ceremony
Stonehaven (31st). *Fireballs are swung about the head up and down the High Street of the old town.*

Highland dancing is only one of many attractions at the Games held all over Scotland during the summer months. This lively trio were at Pitlochry ▼

Atlas

▲ Loch Morar

The following pages contain a legend, key
map and atlas of the Scottish Highlands,
five motor tours and fourteen planned
walks in the Highlands countryside.

MAP SYMBOLS

THE GRID SYSTEM

The map references used in this book are based on the Ordnance Survey National Grid, correct to within 1000 metres. They comprise two letters and four figures, and are preceded by the atlas page number.

Thus the reference for Inverness appears 88 NH 6645

88 is the atlas page number

NH identifies the major (100km) grid square concerned (see diag)

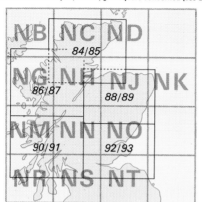

6645 locates the lower left-hand corner of the kilometre grid square in which Inverness appears.

Take the first figure of the reference 6, this refers to the numbered grid running along the bottom of the page.
Having found this line, the second figure 6, tells you the distance to move in tenths to the right of this line. A vertical line through this point is the first half of the reference.

The third figure 4, refers to the numbered grid lines on the right hand side of the page, finally the fourth figure 5, indicates the distance to move in tenths above this line. A horizontal line drawn through this point to intersect with the first line gives the precise location of the places in question.

ATLAS 1:500,000–1" TO 8 MILES ROAD INFORMATION

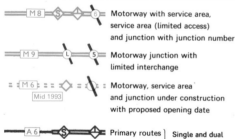

Motorway with service area, service area (limited access) and junction with junction number

Motorway junction with limited interchange

Motorway, service area and junction under construction with proposed opening date

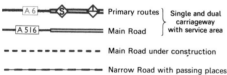

Primary routes } Single and dual carriageway with service area

Main Road }

Main Road under construction

Narrow Road with passing places

other roads { B roads (majority numbered)
Unclassified (selected)

Gradient (1 in 7 and steeper) and toll

Primary routes and main roads

Motorways

Mileages are shown on the map between large markers and between small markers in large and small type

1 mile = 1·61 kilometres

Motorways

A similar situation occurs with motorway routes where numbers and mileages, shown in blue on these maps correspond to the blue background of motorway road signs.

Primary Routes

These form a national network of recommended through routes which complement the motorway system. Selected places of major traffic importance are known as Primary Route Destinations and are shown on these maps thus DUNDEE. This relates to the directions on road signs which on Primary Routes have a green background. To travel on a Primary Route, follow the direction to the next Primary Destination shown on the green backed road signs. On these maps Primary Route road numbers and mileages are shown in green.

WATER FEATURES

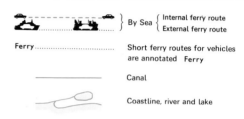

By Sea { Internal ferry route
External ferry route

Ferry .... Short ferry routes for vehicles are annotated Ferry

——————— Canal

Coastline, river and lake

GENERAL FEATURES

——————— Railway

AA...A   RAC...R   PO...T   Telephone call box

+–+–+–+–+–+–+–+–+–+ National Boundary

– – – – – – – – – – – – County or Region Boundary

✈   o   Large Town   Town / Village

⊕ .... Airport

427, ... Height (metres)

TOURS

2 🚗   Start point of tour

➡   Direction of tour

▬▬▬   Featured tour

⑥   Point of Interest

TOURIST INFORMATION

Ⲗ   Camp Site
⚲   Caravan Site
ℹ   Information Centre
🅿   Parking Facilities
※   Viewpoint
✕   Picnic site
⚑   Golf course or links
🏰   Castle
⌂   Cave
🎋   Country park
✿   Garden
🏛   Historic house
🌿   Nature reserve
☆   Other tourist feature
🚂   Preserved railway
🏇   Racecourse
🐾   Wildlife park
🏛   Museum
🍂   Nature or forest trail
𝔪   Ancient monument
☏ ☏   Telephones : public or motoring organisations
PC   Public Convenience
▲   Youth Hostel

80

TOURS 1:250,000 – ¼" TO 1 MILE ROADS AND RAILWAYS

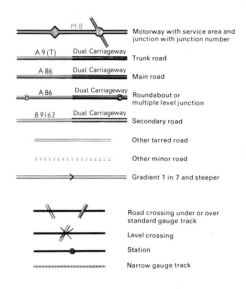

Motorway with service area and junction with junction number

A 9 (T) — Dual Carriageway — Trunk road

A 86 — Dual Carriageway — Main road

A 86 — Dual Carriageway — Roundabout or multiple level junction

B 9163 — Dual Carriageway — Secondary road

Other tarred road

Other minor road

Gradient 1 in 7 and steeper

Road crossing under or over standard gauge track

Level crossing

Station

Narrow gauge track

WATER FEATURES

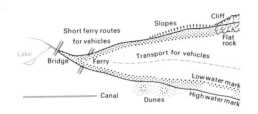

Lake — Short ferry routes for vehicles — Slopes — Cliff — Flat rock — Transport for vehicles — Bridge — Ferry — Low water mark — Canal — Dunes — High water mark

GENERAL FEATURES

Buildings

⊕ Civil aerodrome (with custom facilities)

Wood

Ⴧ Radio or TV mast

Lighthouse

ſ ſ Telephones : public or motoring organisations

ANTIQUITIES

≈ Native fortress

------ Roman road (course of)

Castle • Other antiquities

CANOVIVM • Roman antiquity

RELIEF

Feet	Metres	
		.274
		Heights in feet above mean sea level
3000	914	
2000	610	
1400	427	
		Contours at 200 ft intervals
1000	305	
600	183	
200	61	
		To convert feet to metres multiply by 0.3048
0	0	

WALKS

Start point of walk — Line of walk

Direction of walk — Alternative route

③ Point of interest

WALKS 1:25,000 – 2½" TO 1 MILE ROADS, RAILWAYS AND PATHS

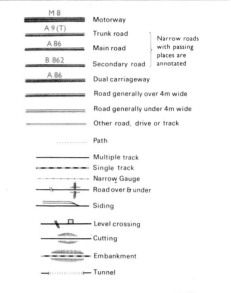

M 8 — Motorway

A 9 (T) — Trunk road

A 86 — Main road — ⎱ Narrow roads with passing places are annotated

B 862 — Secondary road

A 86 — Dual carriageway

Road generally over 4m wide

Road generally under 4m wide

Other road, drive or track

.... Path

Multiple track

Single track

Narrow Gauge

Road over & under

Siding

Level crossing

Cutting

Embankment

Tunnel

GENERAL FEATURES

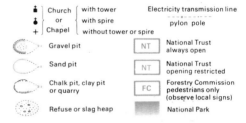

Church — with tower
or — with spire
Chapel — without tower or spire

Electricity transmission line
pylon pole

Gravel pit

Sand pit

Chalk pit, clay pit or quarry

Refuse or slag heap

NT — National Trust always open

NT — National Trust opening restricted

FC — Forestry Commission pedestrians only (observe local signs)

National Park

HEIGHTS AND ROCK FEATURES

Contours are at various metres / feet vertical intervals

50 · ⎱ Determined ⎰ ground survey
285 · ⎰ by ⎱ air survey

Surface heights are to the nearest metre / foot above mean sea level. Heights shown close to a triangulation pillar refer to the station height at ground level and not necessarily to the summit .

Vertical Face

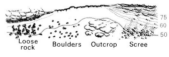

75
60
50

Loose rock — Boulders — Outcrop — Scree

RIGHTS OF ACCESS

There is no law of trespass in Scotland. However landowners can and do impose restrictions on access such as during the grouse shooting season. They also have a legal remedy against any person causing damage on or to their land and may use reasonable force to remove such a person.

The following simple guidelines should therefore be followed :
Obey restricted access notices and if asked to leave please do so.
Always take care to avoid damage to property and the natural environment.
Common sense, care and courtesy are the watchwords.

The representation on this map of any other road, track or path is no evidence of the existence of a right of access.

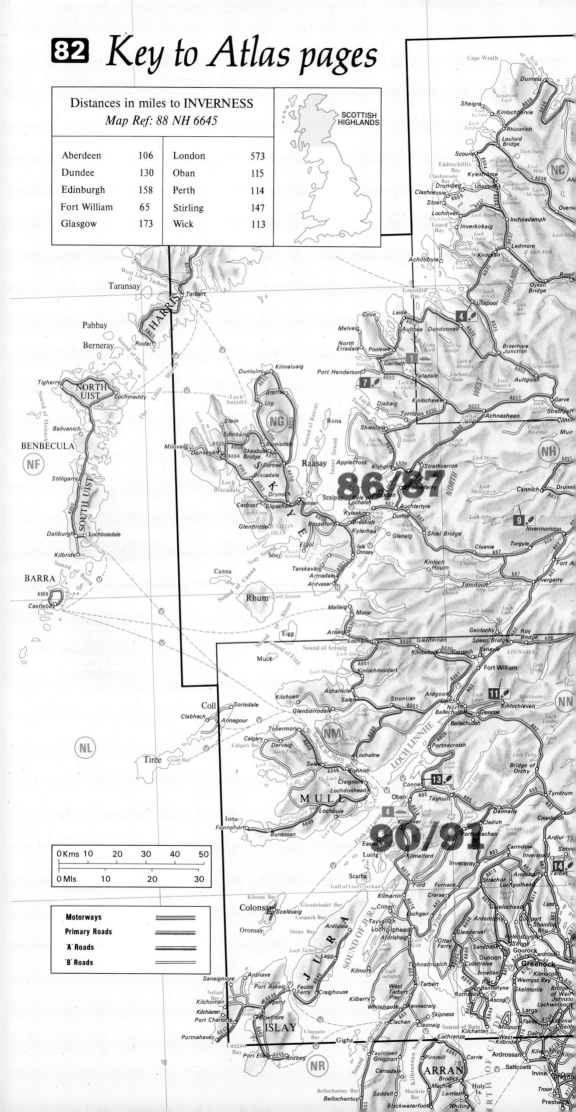

82 Key to Atlas pages

Distances in miles to INVERNESS
Map Ref: 88 NH 6645

Aberdeen	106	London	573
Dundee	130	Oban	115
Edinburgh	158	Perth	114
Fort William	65	Stirling	147
Glasgow	173	Wick	113

SCOTTISH HIGHLANDS

| Motorways |
| Primary Roads |
| 'A' Roads |
| 'B' Roads |

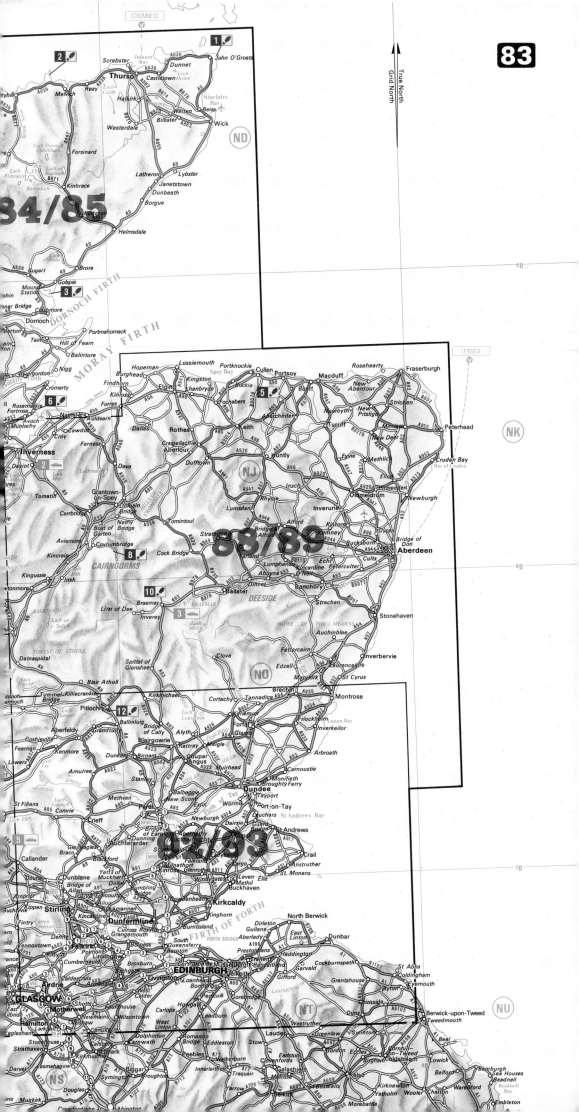

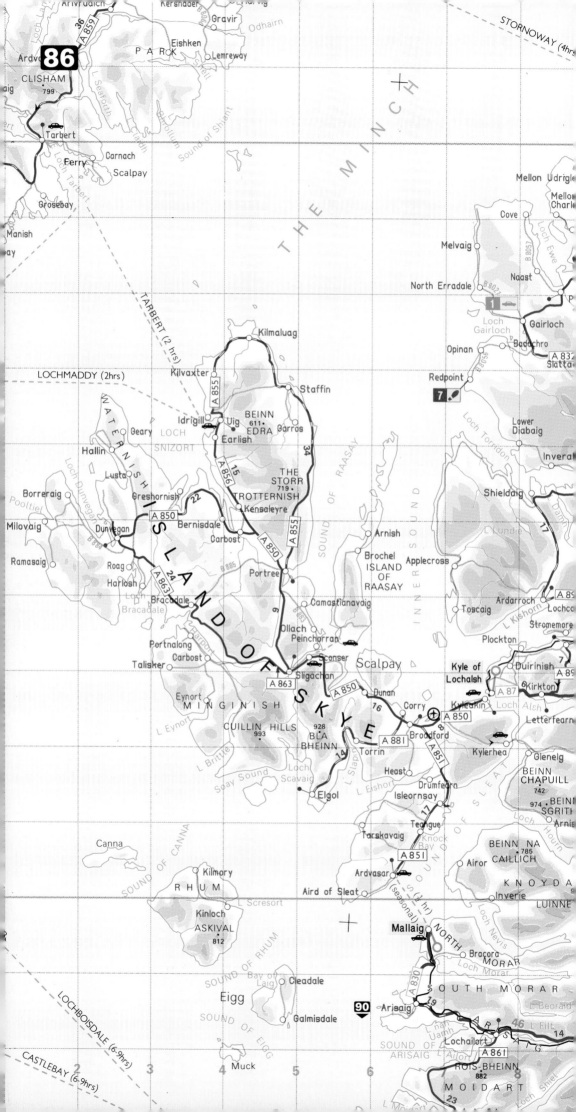

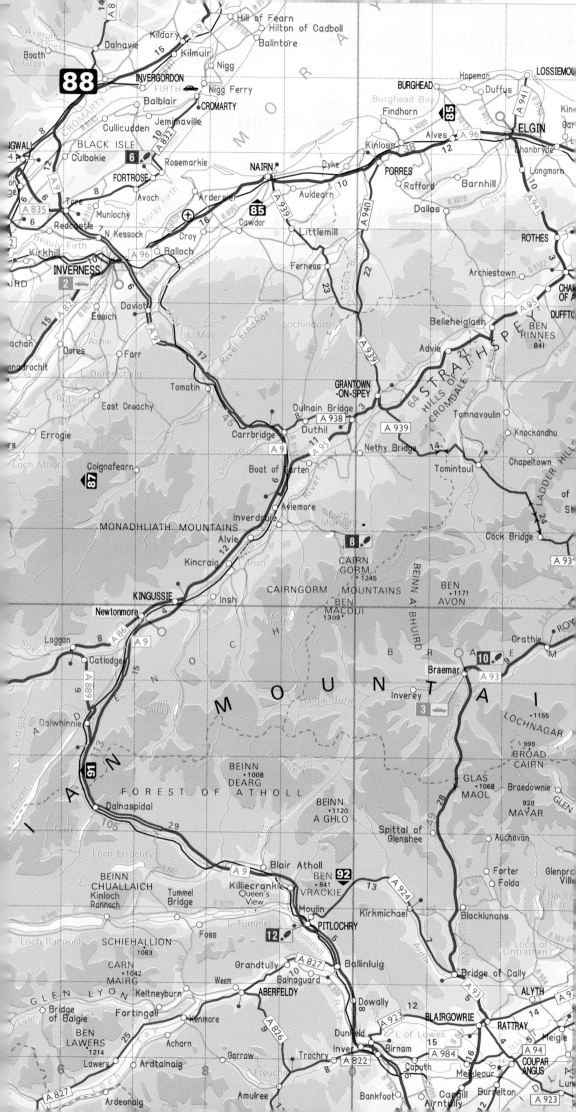

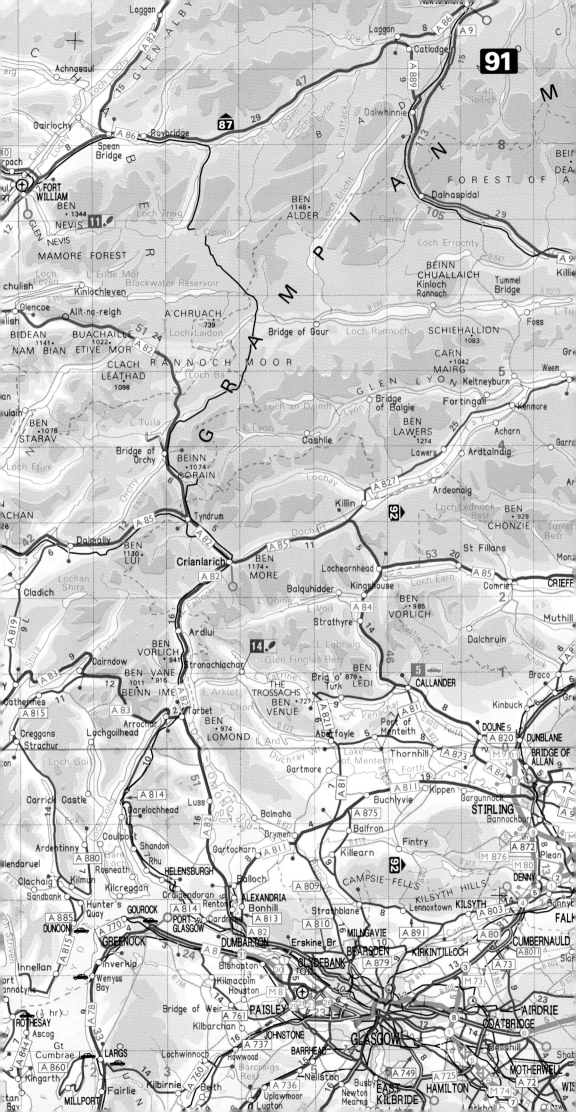

TOUR 1

LOCHS, FORESTS AND FALLS

From Gairloch, the tour runs down the beautiful, island-studded Loch Maree, then inland by Strath Bran past several other fine lochs to swing north to the dramatic Corrieshalloch Gorge and past Little Loch Broom, Gruinard Bay and the famous Inverewe Gardens to return to Gairloch.

ROUTE DIRECTIONS

The drive starts from Gairloch ①. 108 miles.

Leave Gairloch village by the A832 Kinlochewe road. The road follows the course of the River Kerry past Loch Bad an Sgalaig to reach Slattadale Forest and Loch Maree ②.

Parts of this first section are single-track: please drive with due care and use passing places to permit overtaking. The delightful Victoria Falls (named after the Queen, who stayed here in 1877) can be viewed by a simple, short walk from Slattadale.

Continue along Loch Maree to Kinlochewe, passing the Beinn Eighe Visitor Centre ③.

At Kinlochewe, continue on the A832 (again, partly single-track) through the dramatic defile of Glen Docherty and past Loch a'Chroisg to Achnasheen, where the Kyle of Lochalsh road joins from the right. Continue along Strath Bran to Loch Luichart ④.

At Gorstan turn left on to the A835 (signed Ullapool). On the right is Ben Wyvis, standing at 3,433ft. After Garbat the road steadily climbs to pass Loch Glascarnoch, a reservoir forming part of the hydroelectric power system, and drops across the Dirrie More down to Braemore Junction, where there is a car park for the Corrieshalloch Gorge ⑤.

Turn left, back on to the A832 (signed Gairloch). In a mile, a high viewpoint gives a superb view down Loch Broom towards Ullapool. The road drops down again past Dundonnell, with the magnificent An Teallach (The Forge, 3,484ft) towering above, and runs alongside Little Loch Broom before reaching Gruinard Bay with its infamous island ⑥.

The road soon reaches Loch Ewe, with more lovely coastal scenery, and just before Poolewe, it passes Inverewe Gardens ⑦.

From Poolewe it is 5 miles back to Gairloch. On the way, there is another superlative view, down the full length of Loch Maree.

▲ Gairloch

① Gairloch has lovely sandy beaches and a glorious situation on Loch Gairloch, looking out towards Skye and the Outer Isles. Housed in a converted farmstead, the Heritage Museum has won awards for its presentation of life in the West Highlands, from prehistoric times to the present day. South of Gairloch, a 9-mile drive leads to another superb view from Red Point, start of Walk 7.

② Loch Maree is renowned for its beauty. It has a number of wooded islands, on one of which is said to be the burial place of St Maelrubha, from whom the loch takes its name. The view down the loch is dominated by Slioch, standing at 3,215ft, a superbly-shaped mountain with a steep west face.

③ A mile north of Kinlochewe is the visitor centre for the Beinn Eighe National Nature Reserve. Owned by Scottish Natural Heritage (formerly the Nature Conservancy Council for Scotland), this was the first NNR in Britain and is noted for its wildlife and ancient woodland. It has been awarded the Diploma of the Council of Europe for the high standard of conservation management. There are two trails for visitors, and the centre has displays and literature.

④ Loch Luichart – which has its own railway station – is one of a number of lochs in this area used for generating hydroelectric power. There is a power station at Grudie Bridge, at the west end of the loch, which also takes power from Loch Fannich, some miles to the north.

⑤ The Corrieshalloch Gorge, a National Nature Reserve owned by the National Trust for Scotland, is a mile-long box canyon 200ft deep, carved out during the last Ice Age. The sheer sides are hung with lichens and mosses. A suspension bridge designed by J W Fowler (one of the team responsible for another wonder of Scotland, the Forth Rail Bridge) provides an amazing overhead view of the 150ft Falls of Measach as they plunge into the canyon.

⑥ The broad sweep of Gruinard Bay is blessed with lovely sandy beaches. In the bay is Gruinard Island, used for experiments in germ warfare, using anthrax, during World War II. It has only very recently been declared safe again. From a viewpoint high above the west side of the bay you look across the island to Beinn Ghoblach and the hills of Inverpolly.

⑦ Inverewe Garden was created by Osgood Mackenzie, Laird of Gairloch, from an expanse of bare rock and poor soil over 100 years ago. Its exposed position caught the gales and was regularly drenched in sea-spray. But the planting of a shelterbelt of pine trees allowed the garden to take full advantage of the close proximity of the Gulf Stream, enabling it to grow rare and sub-tropical plants. The exotic plants and trees include many from South America, together with Himalayan lilies, and giant forget-me-nots from the South Pacific. The garden is open all year and the National Trust for Scotland visitor centre is open from April to September. It has a shop, restaurant, caravan and camp site, and you can join guided walks round the garden.

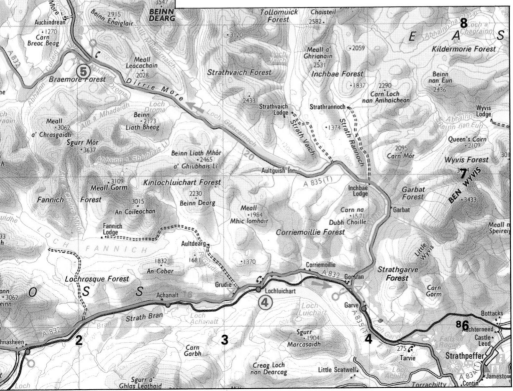

TOUR 2

MONSTERS AND MYSTERIES

From Inverness this tour circumnavigates the mysterious waters of Loch Ness, visiting Drumnadrochit's Loch Ness Monster Exhibitions and Urquhart Castle, and finishes by running down Strathnairn to take in Clava Cairns and Culloden.

ROUTE DIRECTIONS

The drive starts from Inverness ①.
95 miles.

Follow signs for Fort William to leave Inverness by the A82 and keep on this road as it runs down the west side of Loch Ness ②.
  After 15 miles the road reaches Drumnadrochit ③.
  The route continues, still on the A82, with superb views across the loch, and passes through Invermoriston to reach Fort Augustus ④.
  Leave Fort Augustus by the B862 (signed Errogie and Foyers). The roads on this side of Loch Ness are single-track in places: please drive with care and use passing places to permit overtaking. The road – using the line engineered by General Wade — climbs steeply past Loch

Tarff. At its summit there is a magnificent view ahead down Strath Errick. Pass through Whitebridge and in 1 mile fork left on the B852 to reach Foyers ⑤.
  Continue for a further 3 miles to Inverfarigaig. Turn right past the forest visitor centre and continue up the dramatic Pass of Farigaig to Errogie. Turn left on the B862 and in 2 miles fork right on the B851 (signed Daviot) for the lovely run down Strathnairn ⑥.
  At Daviot, turn left on to the A9 and in 1 mile turn right (signed Croy). In 4 miles, at a crossroads, turn right downhill and follow signs to Clava Cairns ⑦.
  Return to the crossroads, go straight over, and in ¼ mile turn left on the B9006 to return to Inverness, passing the NTS visitor centre at Culloden ⑧.

POINTS OF INTEREST

① Inverness, rightly known as the capital of the Highlands, is a busy place with excellent shopping. The city's sandstone castle is 19th century and across the River Ness, next door to modern Eden Court Theatre, is its contemporary, St Andrew's Cathedral. Castle and cathedral can be linked by a fine riverside walk passing over the Ness Islands.
② Loch Ness is a vast basin gouged out by glaciers during the last Ice Age. It is 24 miles long and in places is over 700ft deep. The loch never freezes. Loch Ness is part of the Caledonian Canal system, but its main claim to fame is of course its fabled occupant, Nessie. Sightings of the 'monster' have been reported for centuries, but the truth is still elusive.
③ Drumnadrochit (the name means 'ridge of the bridge') has not one, but two exhibitions devoted to Nessie. After visiting them, drive a mile south to Urquhart Castle, a favourite 'monster watching' point, and see if anything emerges from the depths. Urquhart, impressively sited on a headland, dates from the 14th century but was extensively damaged in 1692 during the Jacobite Rebellions.
④ Fort Augustus was one of the links in the command chain set up by General George Wade in the troubled times of the early 18th century. Four of Wade's roads meet here. The Abbey (now a school) occupies the site of the fort; Wade also stationed a galley here to patrol the loch – looking for rebels, not monsters.
  There is a very pleasant short walk beside the locks on the Caledonian Canal, which in summer are busy with pleasure craft.
⑤ Foyers was the first place in Scotland to have a commercial hydroelectric power station. Opened in 1896, it is still used for this purpose today. The water power orginally came from the Falls of Foyers (a short walk from the village) and was used to produce aluminium, but today a major pumped-storage scheme, using water from Loch Mhor, produces electricity for the grid. A diversion (signed Lower Foyers) leads to the lochside and power station.
⑥ From Errogie to Daviot the route runs down Strathnairn, a beautiful glen that is happily off the well-beaten tourist track on the A9. The glen is fertile with many farms and wooded hills. A 1-mile leftward diversion from Croachy leads to Loch Ruthven, a nature reserve run by the Royal Society for the Protection of Birds. The rare black-throated diver nests here.
⑦ Clava Cairns, tucked away in the shadow of the impressive railway viaduct spanning Strathnairn, is a superb collection of prehistoric burial mounds and standing stones with an extraordinarily evocative atmosphere. There is, quite rightly, no visitor centre or other facilities; discreet signboards tell as much as we know and the stones are left to speak for themselves.
⑧ In contrast with Clava, Culloden has an excellent visitor centre with a fine interpretive display and an audio-visual programme explaining the events leading up to the tragic battle of 16 April 1745, the last stand by the Jacobites against Government forces. The battlefield itself contains memorial stones to the clans who fought here and also shows where Cumberland's troops were positioned.

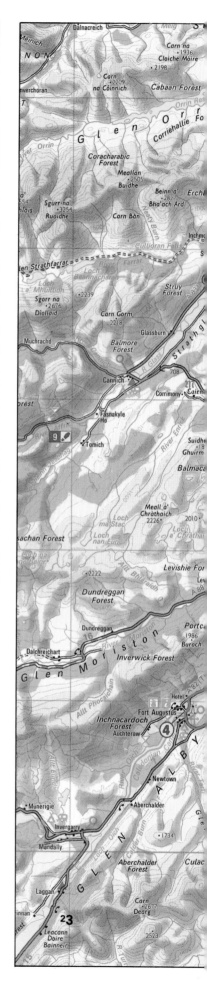

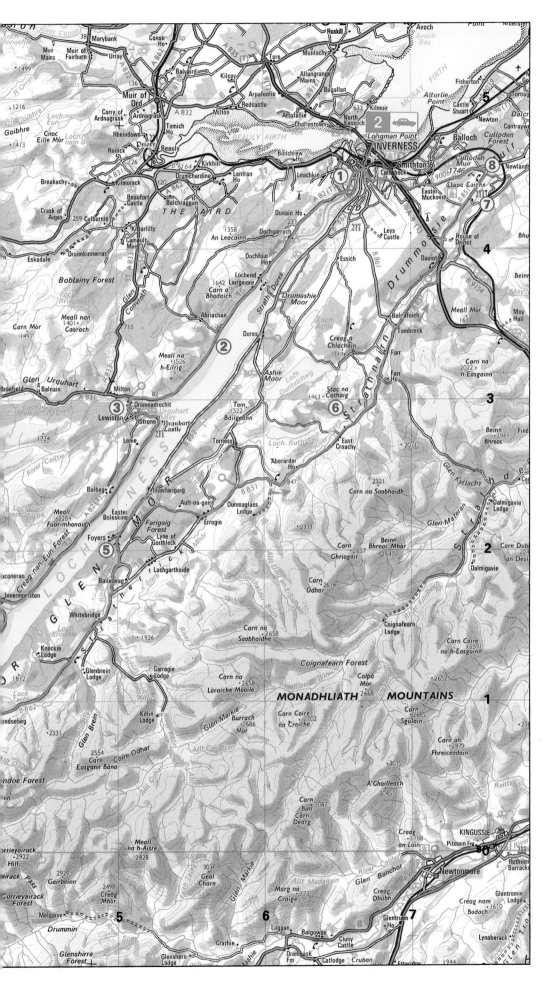

TOUR 3

BY DEE AND DON

Leaving Braemar, the tour follows Royal Deeside through Balmoral and Ballater before heading north to Alford and then west. The upper reaches of the River Don are followed to historic Corgarff before the return to Braemar. A feast of fine scenery and six castles – what more could you ask for?

ROUTE DIRECTIONS

The drive starts from Braemar ①.
84 miles.

Leave Braemar by the A93 Aberdeen road. In 1 mile pass Braemar Castle and in 9 miles reach Balmoral ②.

Continue on the A93, following the lovely Dee valley to the town of Ballater, formerly the railway terminus ③.

In another 4 miles, turn left on to the A97 (signed Huntly). On the left here is the Muir of Dinnet nature reserve ④.

In 3 miles, where the A97 turns left, go ahead on the B9119 and continue through Tarland. There are fine views back towards Deeside. In 6 miles after Tarland, turn left on to the A980 and follow the signs to Craigievar Castle ⑤.

From Craigievar, return to the A980 and turn left. A mile before Alford – which has a working steam railway – turn left on to

the A944 for 6 miles and then left again on to the A97. In 3 miles reach Kildrummy Castle ⑥.

Continue on the A97 past Glenbuchat Castle, a 16th-century, Z-plan, fortified house once the home of the noted Jacobite John Gordon, known as 'Old Glenbucket'. In another 2 miles turn right on to the A944 to drive up the splendid upper valley of the Don, with high hills all around. In 8 miles turn right on to the A939 (signed Tomintoul) for 2 miles to reach Corgarff Castle ⑦.

Return to Colnabaichin and turn right on to the A939 (signed Ballater), leaving Strathdon to climb over a high pass into Glen Gairn. Turn right on to the B976 (single track road) for 5 miles to Crathie, where the Royal Family worship while staying at Balmoral. Turn right on to the A93 and return to Braemar.

POINTS OF INTEREST

① Braemar is one of the highest villages in Scotland. Tucked into a junction of glens, it is a noted frost hollow and jointly holds the record for the lowest temperature recorded in Britain at −27.2°C. It was formerly two villages, Auchendryne and Castleton, and the old castle of Kindrochit can be seen at the car park off the A93. The newer and much grander Braemar Castle, seat of the Farquharson family, is open to visitors in summer. The famous Braemar Gathering, regularly attended by members of the Royal Family, takes place on the first Saturday in September.

② Queen Victoria and Prince Albert first visited Deeside in 1848, and fell in love with the area immediately. On the way south, after that first visit, the Queen recorded that 'the English coast appears terribly flat'. They bought Balmoral in 1852, demolished the former house and had the present grand mansion, designed by William Smith, city architect of Aberdeen, built in its place. It has been the Scottish home for the Royal Family ever since.

③ Ballater was developed in the latter part of the 18th century as a spa after the discovery of supposedly beneficial waters at Pannanich – the Pannanich Wells Hotel is still there, contrasting with the modern timeshare resort at Craigendarroch (crag of oaks) north of the town. Royal visitors regularly came by train until the line closed in the 1960s. Ballater is a busy holiday town with good shops and many fine walks.

④ The Muir of Dinnet, east of Ballater, is a National Nature Reserve noted for its kames and kettle-holes – features of glacial action in past ages. The largest 'hole' is the Burn o'Vat, an extraordinary landscape feature well worth seeing. The two lochs of Davan and Kinord hold many birds, and otters are also regularly seen here.

⑤ Craigievar Castle (NTS) is a superb example of a fortified tower house, richly embellished inside by its founder, the wealthy merchant William Forbes, whose dealings with Europe earned him the nickname of 'Danzig Willie'. The castle dates from the early 17th century and has exterior harling in a pale apricot colour. The Great Hall has magnificent plasterwork.

⑥ Kildrummy provides a contrast with Craigievar. The first castle here was started by Alexander II in 1228. It was fired in the early 14th century, restored, and captured by David II in 1363. The Earls of Mar did not succeed in reclaiming it until 1626; it was an important stronghold in the 1715 Rising, led by the Earl of Mar, but was largely dismantled shortly afterwards and is now a dramatic ruin.

⑦ Corgarff is another tower house in a magnificent situation commanding upper Strathdon and the high Lecht Road from Tomintoul and Strathspey. Built in about 1530 by the Elphinstone family, it saw action in Montrose's campaign of 1645 and was used in both the 1715 and 1745 Risings. In 1748, Corgarff was taken over by Government forces, who recognised its strategic importance. Two wings and a star-shaped surround were added, and a garrison was stationed here for many years.

The castle underwent much restoration under its then owners, Sir Ernest and Lady Stockdale, before passing into the hands of Historic Scotland.

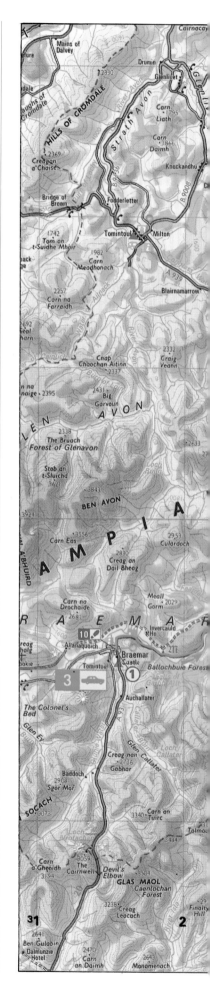

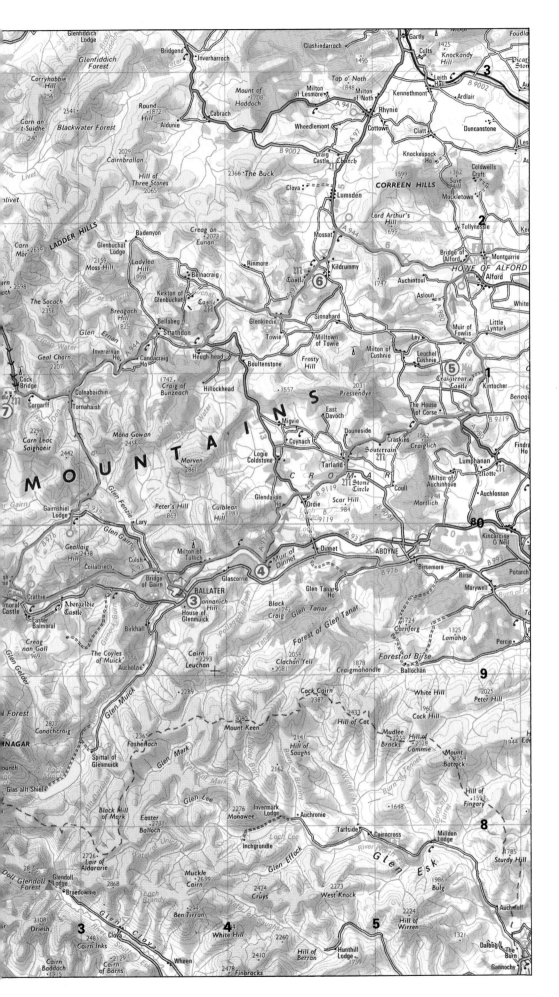

TOUR 4

RANNOCH MOOR AND GLEN COE

Leaving Oban, the tour climbs up to the forbidding Pass of Brander, crosses desolate Rannoch Moor and goes through historic Glen Coe before returning – past many castle ruins – to Loch Linnhe and back to Oban.

ROUTE DIRECTIONS

The drive starts from Oban ①. *102 miles.*

Follow signs for Crianlarich to leave by the A85. After 3 miles the road to the left leads to ruined Dunstaffnage Castle ②.

Later, on the approach to Connel, the Falls of Lora can be seen below Connel Bridge. Continue beside the loch to Taynuilt. A 1½-mile detour may be taken from here to the 18th-century Bonawe Iron Furnace; at the crossroads turn left on to the B845, signed Village, and in ½ mile turn right, unclassified ③.

The main tour continues with the Crianlarich road, A85. Beyond Taynuilt, twin-peaked Ben Cruachan (3,695ft) rises to the left of the road. The drive then enters the wild Pass of Brander and later, on the left, are the Falls of Cruachan below the Cruachan Reservoir ④.

The road continues alongside Loch Awe and after 2¾ miles it passes the church of St Conan. Later, beyond Loch Awe post office, there are views of the ruins of Kilchurn Castle (Ancient Monument) ⑤.

Pass Dalmally, then 2 miles farther, turn left on to the B8074, signed Glen Orchy. The road passes through forested valley scenery featuring several waterfalls. (An easier, alternative route to Bridge of Orchy is via the A85 to Tyndrum, then left on to the A82; it is 5 miles longer.)

After 10¼ miles on the B8074 turn left on to the A82, signed Fort William, and continue to Bridge of Orchy. Beyond the village the road passes Loch Tulla then

climbs on to the bleak bog and lochan waste of Rannoch Moor. The road eventually descends into rugged Glen Coe, overshadowed by the peaks of Bidean nam Bian, at 3,766ft the highest mountain in Argyll, and its outliers, the Three Sisters. One mile beyond Loch Achtriochtan on the right is the Glen Coe Visitor Centre (NTS) ⑥.

Continue down to Glencoe village ⑦.

From Glencoe follow signs for Oban and Fort William alongside Loch Leven. Pass the edge of Ballachulish and in 1¾ miles, at the roundabout, take the second exit, A828, signed Oban. The road runs beneath the Ballachulish Bridge then past the Ballachulish Hotel. Nearby is a monument to James of the Glen ⑧.

The drive then follows the Appin shore of Loch Linnhe, through Kentallen and Duror, with views of the Ardgour Hills across the loch. Before the drive meets the edge of Loch Creran, Castle Stalker can be seen near Portnacroish ⑨.

The drive continues round the loch to the Sea Life Centre and Marine Aquarium at Barcaldine, with several picnic sites and forest walks along the way ⑩.

Later there are views of Barcaldine Castle to the right ⑪.

Continue through Benderloch, skirting Ardmucknish Bay; from here the Moss of Achnacree can be seen over to the left.

After 2¼ miles cross the cantilevered Connel Bridge. At the T-junction turn left on to the A85 for the return to Oban.

POINTS OF INTEREST

① Oban is a popular resort and the port serving the islands of Mull, Coll, Tiree, Lismore, Colonsay, Barra and South Uist. Of interest around the town are McCaig's Folly, the Oban Glassworks and, a mile to the north-west, the ruins of 13th-century Dunollie Castle.

② Dunstaffnage Castle, guarding the entrance to Loch Etive, dates from the 13th century and has a 17th-century tower-house. The Campbells of Dunstaffnage are buried in the adjacent ruined chapel.

③ Once the main iron-smelting centre of Scotland, Taynuilt provided the cannon and shot for the navy, and a monument near the church commemorates Nelson's victory at Trafalgar. The restored remains of an 18th- to 19th-century furnace can be seen.

④ The Reservoir stands at 1,315ft and the power station is built deep into the mountain. The visitor centre, on the A85, has displays and literature explaining the scheme.

⑤ Kilchurn Castle was built in 1440 by Sir Colin Campbell of Glenorchy. It was extended in 1693 by Ian, Earl of Breadalbane.

⑥ The Centre stands about half a mile from Signal Rock, from which the signal was given for the hideous massacre of the Macdonalds of Glencoe by the Campbells of Glen Lyon in 1692.

⑦ Two heather-thatched cottages in the main street house the Glencoe and North Lorn Folk Museum, with Macdonald and Jacobite relics.

⑧ James of the Glen was wrongly hanged in 1752 after a notorious trial known as the Appin murder case. The story plays a great part in R L Stevenson's novel *Kidnapped*.

⑨ Castle Stalker was built at the beginning of the 16th century and has been well restored. It was the ancient home of the Stewarts of Appin.

⑩ The Sea Life Centre and Marine Aquarium on Loch Creran contains the largest collection of native marine life in Britain.

⑪ Barcaldine Castle was built between 1579 and 1601 by 'Black Duncan' Campbell of Glenorchy. It has been much restored.

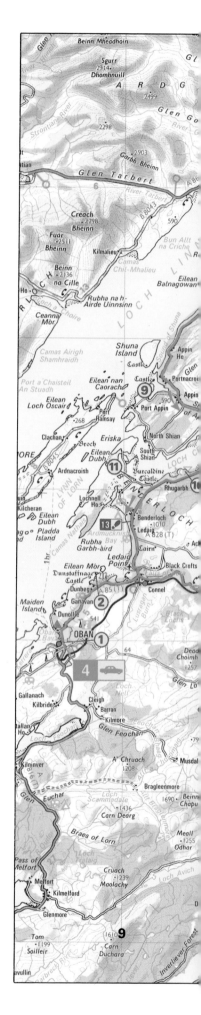

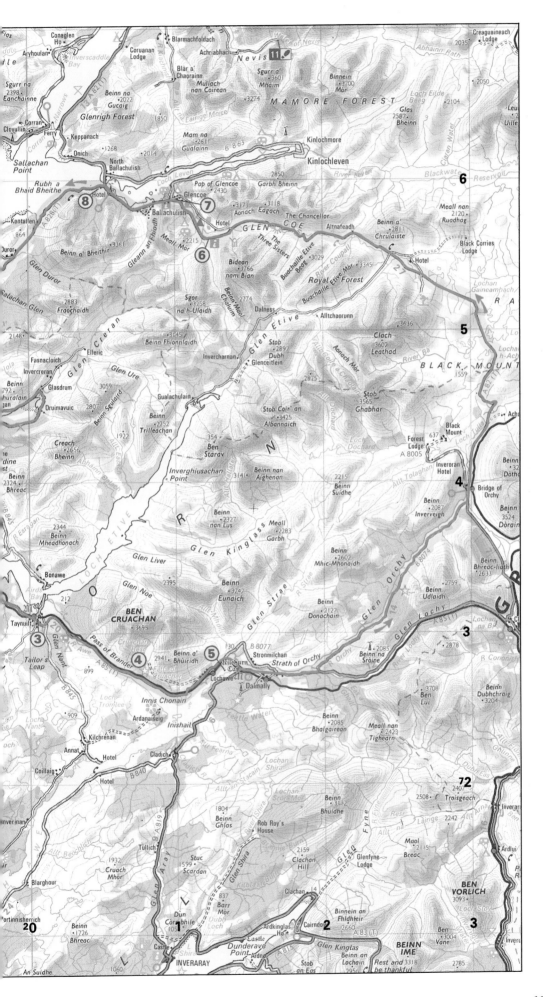

TOUR 5

A TOUCH OF THE TROSSACHS

A short tour of the area made famous by Sir Walter Scott, passing through superb landscapes of mountain, loch and forest.

ROUTE DIRECTIONS

The drive starts from Callander ①. 60 miles.

Leave Callander by the A84, northward, and after 1 mile, at Kilmahog, turn left on to the A821, signed Aberfoyle and The Trossachs ②.

The route then runs above Loch Vennachar, with its rather grand Victorian sluice house, with Ben Ledi rising on the right. This was one of the hills on which ancient people celebrated the Beltane, the coming of spring, by lighting a fire on the summit.

Pass through the hamlet of Brig o'Turk – which, unlike Kilmahog, does signify an association with boars – and continue on past Kennedy's 1849 Trossachs parish church on its hillock to Loch Achray ③.

At a fork, go right for a short distance to the pier on Loch Katrine ④.

Return to the fork and turn right for Aberfoyle. The road climbs steadily over the Duke's Pass, first made by the Duke of Montrose over 100 years ago ⑤.

The road then twists steeply down into the village of Aberfoyle, the first crossing-point on the River Forth. At the junction, turn right on to the B829. Two miles from Aberfoyle the road reaches the shore of Loch Ard ⑥.

Continue through Kinlochard to Inversnaid. After Kinlochard the road narrows to single-track – please drive with due care and use passing places to let others overtake. The road winds on past Loch Chon (loch of the dog) and Loch Arklet, and finally plunges down to arrive at Inversnaid on the shores of Loch Lomond ⑦.

Return towards Aberfoyle, but at the far end of Loch Arklet turn left over a cattle grid to Stronachlachar ⑧.

Return to Loch Arklet, turn left and continue to Aberfoyle. At the crossroads join the A821 (straight ahead), pass through Aberfoyle, and in 1 mile bear left on the A81 for the return journey to Callander. After 5 miles pass the Lake of Menteith ⑨.

POINTS OF INTEREST

① Callander is a busy tourist town with an attractive riverside park. The Rob Roy Centre tells the story of Rob Roy MacGregor and of tourism in the Trossachs.

② Kilmahog has nothing to do with wild boar; the name means 'cell of St Chug', one of the many Celtic saints. The two woollen mills here are popular stopping places.

③ Loch Achray is in the heart of the Trossachs. As befits the wild architectural extravagance of the Trossachs Hotel, it was designed by a man whose name could easily have come from one of Scott's romances – Lord Willoughby d'Eresby. The hotel was built in 1852 to cater for the many tourists already visiting the area.

④ In summer, there are boat trips down Loch Katrine on the SS Sir Walter Scott – a lovely cruise passing Ellen's Isle, made famous in the epic poem *The Lady of the Lake*, the publication of which, in 1810, started the whole tourist business here. It was a blockbuster of its day.

⑤ There are several car parks and viewpoints on the Duke's Pass, and the Achray Forest Drive – 7 miles through trees and by small lochs – starts here. A mile before Aberfoyle is the David Marshall Lodge, a visitor centre run by the Forestry Commission with displays on the natural and social history of the area and with attractive short walks laid out.

⑥ Loch Ard has a famous and much-photographed view west to Ben Lomond. At the far end of the loch, on the right, is the Forest Hills timeshare complex and a little further on the handsome farm of Ledard, which usually has many goats around it. This is the start of the path up Ben Venue, a favourite Trossachs walk.

⑦ There is another grand Victorian hotel at Inversnaid and the West Highland Way path passes through the town. A short stop can be made to admire the fine waterfall, celebrated in verse by both Wordsworth and Gerard Manley Hopkins. Government troops were stationed in the barracks here during the Risings of the 18th century.

⑧ This is the west end of Loch Katrine, and Stronachlachar (it means headland of the mason) is a water department settlement with a number of pleasant houses. The loch was greatly enlarged about 100 years ago to provide water for Glasgow. Walk 14 starts from here: the area has many associations with Rob Roy MacGregor.

⑨ The name of the Lake of Menteith may come from an old Scots word 'laigh' meaning low-lying. The lake is famous for its birdlife and in hard winters has staged the Grand Match, when hundreds of curlers take to the ice for a day's sport (and not a little imbibing of warming spirit). On the small island of Inchmahome is a 13th-century Augustinian priory. There are regular boat trips to it in summer.

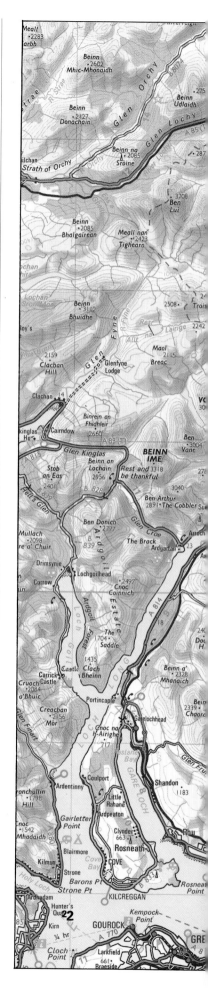

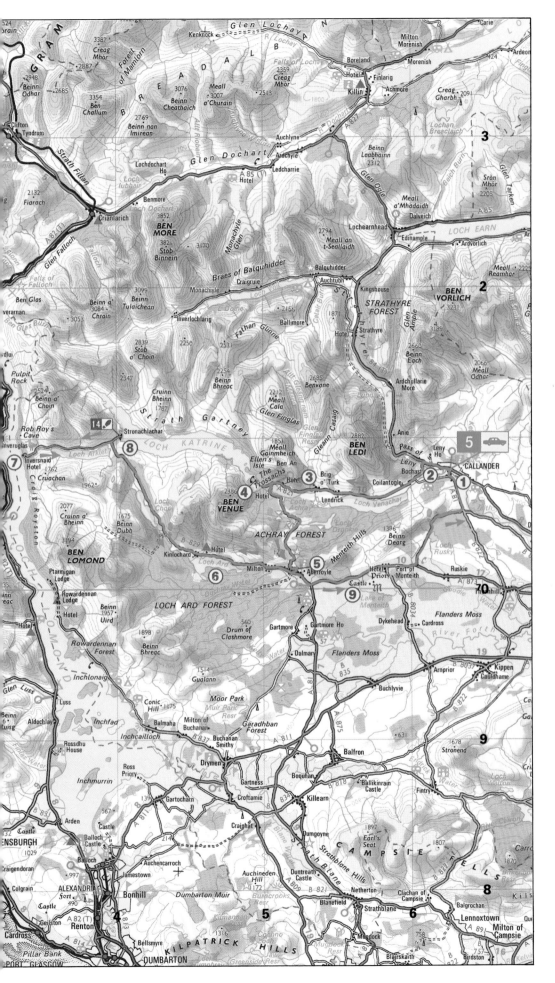

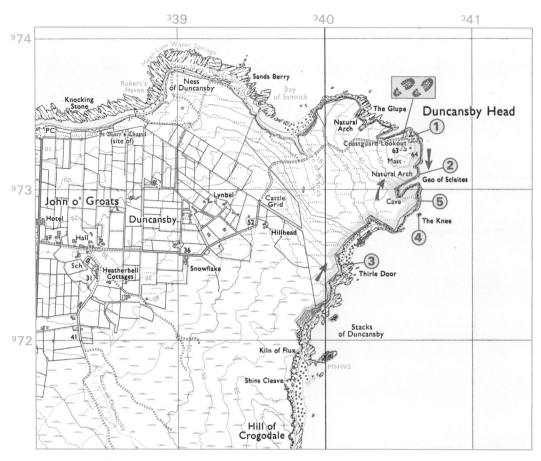

▲ Sea stacks at Duncansby Head

WALK 1

DUNCANSBY HEAD

This easy walk starts at the true north-east corner of the British mainland, 2 miles east of John o'Groats, and gives superb views of the spectacular pyramidic Stacks of Duncansby. The cliff edge is fenced, so the walk is quite safe. Parts of the path are likely to be boggy.

ROUTE DIRECTIONS

Approx. 2½ miles. Allow 1½ hours
Start from the car park at Duncansby Head lighthouse (grid ref. ND404733).

From the car park follow the sign marked 'Footpath to Stacks of Duncansby'. A good information board gives details of birds, cliff flowers, and Sclaites Geo. Walk up to the triangulation pillar near the lighthouse ①.

Continue on the clear grass path to reach the edge of Sclaites Geo, and walk round the geo ②.

Carry on, keeping inside the fence, to a point where you look past Thirle Door – a natural rock arch – to see the Stacks of Duncansby at their best ③.

Continue until, almost above the stacks, a fence bars further progress. Return by the same route, noting the isolated pillar stack known as The Knee ④ and enjoying the wide views over the Pentland Firth ⑤.

POINTS OF INTEREST

① The lighthouse was established in 1924 and is unusual in having a tapering square tower with a castellated parapet and a movable foghorn. Half a dozen other lighthouses are visible from here. Although John o'Groats takes all the glory, this is in fact the true north-eastern tip of the British mainland.
② Sclaites Geo is a spectacular example of the way sea erosion works. From its edge, you look down a sheer drop to the pounding waves over 150ft below. There are geos dotted all along the Caithness coast. The natural arch seen here and at Thirle Door is an early stage in the process.
③ The Stacks of Duncansby are very fine examples of their kind. Stacks are formed when the sea erodes the coast, leaving pillars of harder rock standing clear. From close to, you can see the bedded structure of the Old Red Sandstone that makes up the stacks. The three stacks are – in order of size – Muckle Stack, Peedie Stack and Tom Thumb Stack; the Muckle Stack is almost 300ft high. Seabirds nest on them in considerable numbers.
④ The Knee is an isolated pillar stack, well seen on the return walk. It is relatively recent in creation.
⑤ On the return walk there are superb views across the Pentland Firth to the islands of Orkney, nearby Stroma and Swoma, and west past John o'Groats to Dunnet Head, the most northerly point on the coast, 20 miles away.

▲ The lighthouse station at Strathy Point illuminates the dangers of this stretch of coast

WALK 2

STRATHY POINT

This short walk, all on tarmac, takes you to another lighthouse with superb views and excellent birdlife. The cliff edges are unfenced, so care must be exercised, especially in high winds.

ROUTE DIRECTIONS

Approx. 1½ miles. Allow 1½ hours
Start from the car park at the end of the public road (grid ref. NC827687).

From the car park, walk along the private road, owned by the Northern Lighthouse Board. Leave the gate as you found it. Just before the lighthouse you pass Loch nam Faoileag ①.

Continue to the lighthouse station and walk past it on the right to the green beyond to enjoy the spectacular views ②.

At the beginning of the return walk you can venture to the cliff edge west of the lighthouse. From here you can see a natural rock arch and the large sea-cave, Uamh Mhor ③.

Return to the car park by the road; any other route would involve climbing fences and traversing dangerous cliff edges.

POINTS OF INTEREST

① Lochan nam Faoileag means 'loch of the gulls' and you may well see birds on this attractive small sheet of water. It is, if anything, more notable for the two model lighthouses adorning it!

② Strathy Point thrusts a long way into the Pentland Firth and offers superb views of Orkney, especially Hoy with its high cliffs, and the Caithness coast in both directions. Birds likely to be seen include fulmars, cormorants, guillemots, gannets and Manx shearwaters. The cliff flowers include orchids and the rare *primula scotica*, a primrose of a pinky-purple hue found only in Sutherland, Caithness and Orkney. They should never be picked, of course.

The soils near the cliff edge receive considerable amounts of wind-blown sea-spray, and as a result some of the hollows support a selection of plants usually associated with saltmarshes. Just detached from the mainland is the aptly-named Garbh-eilean – the rough island.

③ From the cliff near the lighthouse you can see into the Uamh Mhor, which simply means 'big cave'. This and the fine natural arch nearby are both early stages of sea erosion which will eventually lead to stacks. A little further south, not visible from the walk, is Uamh nan Con – the cave of the dog.

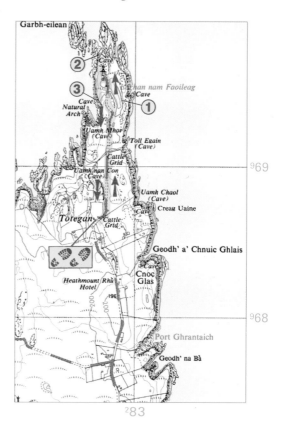

WALK 3

LITTLEFERRY

This walk takes you over a dune system, along a fine stretch of beach, and back through a pine wood beside Loch Fleet. The area is rich in wildlife, and much of it is a Scottish Wildlife Trust reserve.

ROUTE DIRECTIONS

Approx. 4½ miles. Allow 2½ hours
Start from the car park at Littleferry (grid ref. NH806957).

Take the path heading east from the car park and continue along the shore to the point ①.

Turn north and walk towards Golspie. Use the firm sand as far as possible and then go inland a short way to pick up a grassy track. The views are excellent along this stretch ②.

Go left of the go-kart track on a stony track and at the access road turn left. Cross the links, giving way to golfers if necessary, and turn left along the road for about 400yds. At a lay-by with a Scottish Wildlife Trust sign, cross the stile and follow the path through the pines as far as the burn. Do not cross the burn, but keep on the path this side of it. On reaching the sands, cross a fence and join a track to walk along beside the flats of Loch Fleet ③.

Rejoin the road and continue past the car park to the houses and pier at Littleferry ④. Return the short distance along the road to the car park.

POINTS OF INTEREST

① The walk to the point takes you over shingle ridges formed during a period of changing sea levels after the last Ice Age. Across the channel is the mobile dune system of Coul Links. The flow through this narrow channel can be spectacular. You are likely to see eiders and oystercatchers; a rare king eider has been seen here but you will be very lucky to spot it.

② The walk north passes 'Palm Beach', a small remnant group of trees which have survived the marine erosion that killed many of their fellows. The dune front shows both marram and broad-bladed sea lyme grass. Inland, the heathland supports skylarks and, in summer, many butterflies.

The wider view takes in Dunrobin Castle, the ancient seat of the Dukes of Sutherland. Its name derives from Earl Robin, who built the original square keep in the 13th century. It was converted into a château in the 1840s. Also visible, high on Beinn a'Bhragaidh, is the colossal statue to the 1st Duke of Sutherland designed by Sir Francis Chantrey and erected in 1834.

③ Most of the Loch Fleet area is a Scottish Wildlife Trust reserve and the birdlife is rich and varied. The tidal basin attracts numerous wildfowl in winter, including wigeon, goldeneye, eider, red-breasted merganser, and shelduck. Oystercatcher, curlew and knot are also common.

In spring, off the coast, all three divers – common, velvet and occasionally surf scoters – gather and the rare king eider may be spotted. In summer eider and common seal congregate in the estuary. An information board beside the track shows all the species you can expect to see. West of The Mound bridge, the alder woods form another important reserve.

④ Littleferry is a quiet place now, but it was once busy with ferry traffic arriving from Skelbo and further afield carrying coal, lime and other goods as well as passengers. The ice house used for storing fish in winter can still be seen at the back of the former custom house.

In April 1746, a group of Jacobite supporters from Caithness were ambushed and killed here by Loyalist forces as they tried to join the main Jacobite army preparing for the battle of Culloden.

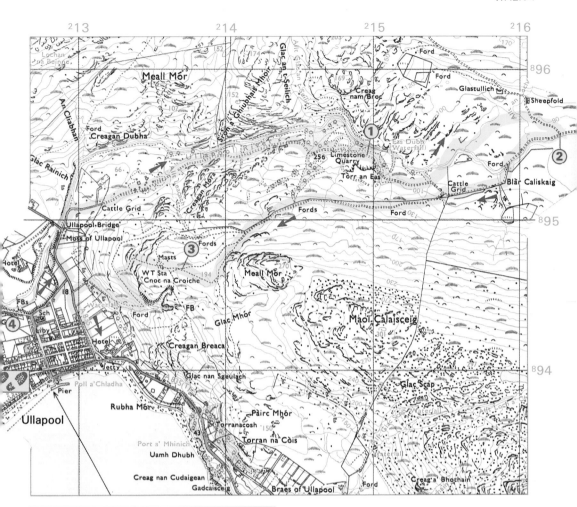

ULLAPOOL TO LOCH ACHALL

After an industrial start, this walk leads to a peaceful inland loch and returns to Ullapool by an old hill track giving fine views.

ROUTE DIRECTIONS

Approx. 5 miles. Allow 2½ hours
The walk starts from the large car park in the centre of Ullapool (grid ref. NH125942).

From the car park, walk back down Latheron Lane and turn left into Quay Street. Swing right with the road (now Riverside Terrace) with good views over the Ullapool River to Loch Broom.

Turn left into Moss Road. Cross the A835 and head uphill on the quarry road opposite, to pass the limestone works and the quarry ①. This part of the walk may be rather noisy, and if blasting is taking place at the quarry please obey instructions. Some large blocks of limestone have been placed by the road, almost as a decoration, and enable you to examine the rock and see how very white it is.

Past the quarry, the views open up. At a fork – where a pony-cart is sometimes parked – go left to cross the river. Pass the driveway to Glastullich and continue ahead to reach Loch Achall ②.

Turn right to start the return walk. Recross the river and use two gates to pass through an enclosure where there is a seasonal wildlife display. About 100yds before the junction where you turned left on the way out, turn left up a rough stony track. As the path climbs, fine views open up to the north ③ and across Loch Broom to Beinn Ghobhlach on the Scoraig Peninsula.

At a fork take the upper path. At a grassy sward go right, aiming for the small building you can see. The path may be wet here. The building, an old GPO radio station, commands splendid views down over Ullapool to the loch and the hills beyond.

From here the path twists steeply downhill. At its end, go through a gate and walk out to the main road. Turn left to explore the quayside and village ④ before returning to the car park.

POINTS OF INTEREST

① Industry such as the quarry and lime-crushing works may spoil the scenery, but are important in an area where opportunities for employment are limited. The quarry is a large and most impressive hole, still being extended uphill and west. The crushed limestone is used for road-building and other construction work where aggregate is required.

② Loch Achall runs inland for 2 miles to Glen Achall. It feeds the Ullapool River, whose short (4-mile), turbulent length is traversed on this walk. On the north side of the river are marked bands of stratified rock, showing how immense forces crushed and twisted the land here aeons ago.

③ Some of the magnificent mountains of wild Sutherland can be glimpsed on the return walk. You can see Cul Mor, Cul Beag and Stac Pollaidh, a popular climb from Loch Lurgainn. These mountains, rising from a flat plain, are among the most dramatic in Britain. You can also see the Summer Isles, which can be visited by boat from Ullapool.

④ Ullapool is a planned village, established in 1788 by the British Fisheries Society, hence the grid pattern of many of its streets. It is still a centre for fisheries, and there are often large factory ships ('klondykers') from Eastern Europe or Russia in the loch. The small museum in Quay Street, run by the Loch Broom Community Association, has much on the area and its history, and there is always plenty to see at the quayside, from where car ferries leave for Stornoway.

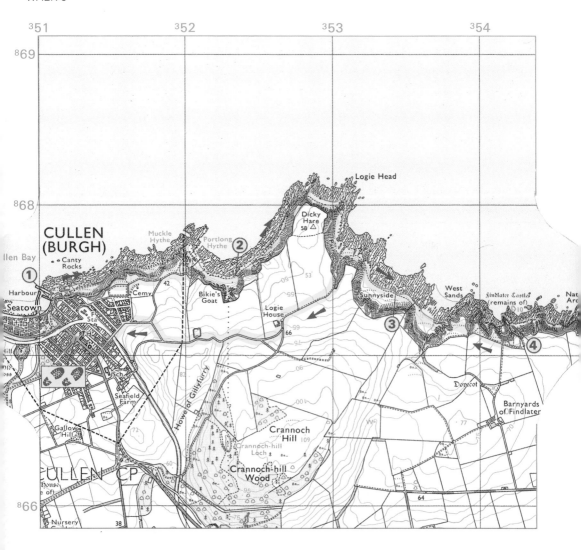

WALK 5

FINDLATER CASTLE

A superb coastal walk from Cullen leads across a lovely sandy bay to the dramatic clifftop ruin of Findlater Castle, with an inland return. Good paths all the way, but care is needed at the castle.

ROUTE DIRECTIONS

Approx. 5 miles. Allow 4 hours
Start from the square in Cullen (grid ref. NJ514671).

From the square, walk down Seafield Street under the railway viaduct to the harbour ①.

Turn right and follow the road, which soon becomes a track, past the old curing-stations and along the foot of the cliff to the former salmon bothy at Portlong ②.

Continue on a lovely path to Logie Head, where you go up and down the Giant's Steps, a superb stone stairway set into the cliff. Continue into Sunnyside Bay ③.

Walk round the bay and at the far end follow the path as it winds up to the top of the cliff. Go through two gateways and continue along the clifftop, enjoying the fine views, for about ½ mile, until Findlater Castle is seen below. Walk down to the castle and explore it – carefully! ④.

For an alternative return route, recross Sunnyside Bay and after the plank bridge over a small burn, turn left up a path to climb the cliff. At the top, almost hidden in a grassy hollow, is an old well with the inscription: 'Rest, Drink and Think. 1895'. It is a good place to do all those things.

Go through the gateway and walk along the edge of the field to the ruined Logie House. Join the farm track heading back towards Cullen, and after about a mile, fork right through a gate, heading down towards the caravan park. Take the next fork left and walk back into Cullen.

POINTS OF INTEREST

① Cullen, often known as 'the pearl of the Banffshire coast', was formerly a fishing community, and to the left of the harbour is the old Seatown, with its small cottages crowded together. Above them soar the viaducts of the former coast railway, built on this line in 1884 when the Countess of Seafield refused to let the trains run past Cullen House, a mile further inland. The railway closed in 1967.

② Net-fishing for salmon was carried out at Portlong from the early 19th century until about 20 years ago, and the fishermen used this bothy. Fishing was the major industry in the area, and 100 years ago there were 90 boats operating from Cullen, with a boatyard sited between the town and Portlong.

③ Sunnyside Bay is a quiet, idyllic place, with no road access. Its broad sandy beach invites you to stop and spend time here. There is always plenty of birdlife, with gulls, fulmars and other seabirds nesting on the cliffs.

④ Findlater Castle seems to have grown out of the cliff rather than being built. It was started in the mid-15th century by Sir Walter Ogilvie, and consists of a living-block on the side of an irregular court. As a fortification it could hardly be bettered. The Ogilvies took the title Earls of Findlater in the 17th century, though by then they had moved to Deskford, leaving the old castle to the wind, waves and the birds. It is a wonderful place to explore, but do take care – there are many holes and the drops are very steep.

WALK 6

ROSEMARKIE

These two short walks with a common start-point will have a special appeal for children, taking in waterfalls, a sandy beach, a cave and a swing-park.

ROUTE DIRECTIONS

Approx. 2 miles for Fairy Glen and 2½ miles for the shore walk. Allow 1 hour and 1½ hours respectively. Start from the burnside car park at the north end of Rosemarkie, off the A832 (grid ref. NH736578).

From the car park, turn right, walk about 80yds to the road bridge and follow the sign for the Fairy Glen. In a further 90yds or so, fork right on to the path that runs into the glen and follow it through the trees, taking care on the small wooden bridges. The path leads past a disused mill-pond to two fine waterfalls ①.

Return by the same route to the car park and, for the second walk, continue on the road for a short distance. Just before the Plough Inn, turn left, cross the burn and walk down beside the football pitch to the swing-park and promenade ②.

At the end of the promenade, climb concrete steps to reach a good path, at first grassy and later sandy, which follows the shore. There is easy access to the beach at several places – this is a very popular walk with dogs as well as children. The walk ends at Caird's Cave under Scart Craig, 1½ miles north of the village. If you go as far as the cave, watch the tide closely, for it is possible to be cut off here, and the water is never warm! ③.

Return by the same route.

POINTS OF INTEREST

① Fairy Glen, a lovely secretive place, is an RSPB reserve holding a variety of birds and many flowers in summer. You may see buzzards circling overhead and dippers busily flying up and down the burn. The path, through ash and sycamore groves, leads to two splendid waterfalls set in natural bowl-shaped amphitheatres, the second one reached by a scramble over a rocky path.
② From the promenade you can look across the Moray

Firth to the squat cubist shape of Fort George, built as part of the moves to quell the Highlands after the 1745–46 Rising. Left of it is the contrasting modern outline of the Ardersier oil-rig fabrication yard. Looking back, the village of Rosemarkie can be seen. You should not leave without visiting Groam House Museum, which has fascinating Pictish artefacts.
③ The shore path is surrounded by a profusion of summer flowers including campion, bloody cranesbill and the delicate burnet rose. Scart Craig has crumbled sandstone pillars and caves, which always fascinate children. The beach shares the same pinkish hue as the cliffs.

Fort George is both an artillery fortress and a full-scale barracks capable of housing 1600 men ▼

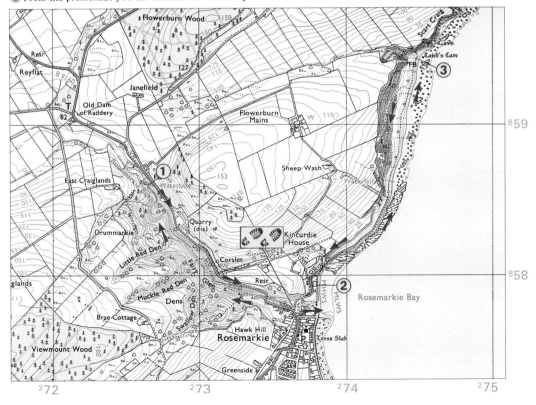

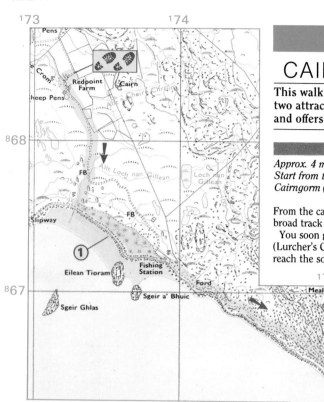

CAIRNGORM LOCHS

This walk in the Glenmore Forest Park passes two attractive lochs – one large, one small – and offers views of the high tops.

ROUTE DIRECTIONS

Approx. 4 miles. Allow 2 hours
Start from the Heron's Field car park on the road to Cairngorm (grid ref. NH981092).

From the car park, follow red waymarks to walk along a broad track through the pine forest ①.
   You soon get a glimpse of Creag an Leth-choin (Lurcher's Crag) high on the left. At the fork go right to reach the southern edge of Loch Morlich ②.

WALK 7

RED POINT

Another superb coastal walk with outstanding views leading to one of Britain's most remote hostels.

ROUTE DIRECTIONS

Approx. 10 miles. Allow 5 hours
Start from the end of the B8056 road at Red Point (grid ref. NG732685). This road offers a fine 9-mile drive from just south of Gairloch.

Park tidily in the space just before Redpoint Farm. In clear conditions you can see the Cuillin of Skye and the Outer Hebrides. Go through a gate, noting the Scottish Rights of Way Society sign 'footpath to Diabaig', and pass the farm on its right.
   Go through two more gates and then cross a very large field, following tractor tyremarks towards a gate in its far right-hand corner. Go through this gate and angle right down towards a beautiful small bay with a lovely sandy beach ①.
   If the tide is suitable, walk along the firm sand to the former fishing station, with its old anchors and netting poles. Go through a gate by the cottage. The path is indistinct at first but after about ⅓ mile it becomes much clearer, making its way along the top of the low cliff.
   Follow this fine old path south, with magnificent seaward views to Raasay, Skye and beyond ②. Partway along, the path climbs higher on the cliff. It crosses several burns, but none provide any great difficulty.
   In 3 miles from the fishing station, reach the Craig River. Follow the path up its north bank for about ⅓ mile, through birch trees and along a lovely gorge, to reach the footbridge leading to Craig Hostel ③.
   Either return by the same route or, as an alternative, head north from the hostel over moorland for 1½ miles to the summit of Meall na h-Uamha, which gives a wonderful panorama of the mountains of Torridon from an unusual angle. From this summit you can drop gradually down to regain the outward path, over ground which is rough and often very wet.

POINTS OF INTEREST

① The bay at Red Point is a gloriously secluded spot and is sometimes used by members of the Royal Family while cruising in the royal yacht *Britannia*. Note that the wee islet is called Eilean Tioram. It means 'dry island', and the islet is linked to the beach at low water.
② The coast path is a walk to savour, with its wonderful seaward views. Birdlife will include cormorants and gulls, and there are almost certainly otters in this area, though you would be very lucky to get a sighting. There is a fine herd of wild goats here too, usually to be found in the rocks above the path.
③ Craig, only accessible on foot, has been a hostel since 1934, three years after the Scottish YHA was formed.

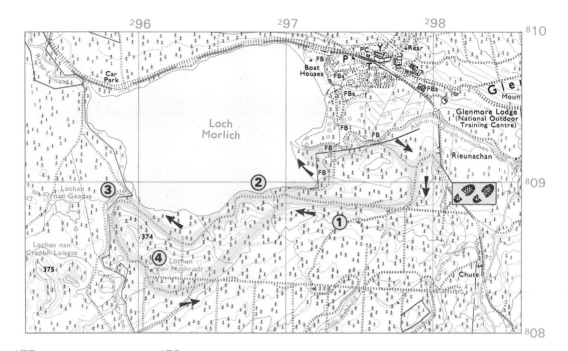

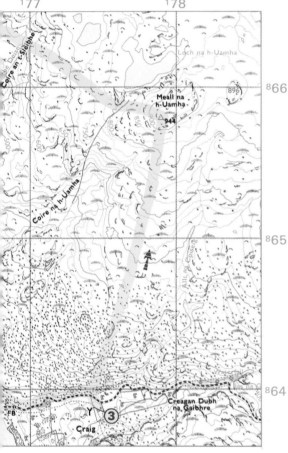

There is a lovely view across the loch to Meall a'Buachaille (the herdsman's hill, 2,660ft). In summer you will see much watersports activity on the loch. At the boundary with the Rothiemurchus Estate ③ swing left, away from the loch.

The view ahead opens up to take in the ski area in Coire Cas, with the summit of Cairngorm above it. At a sign, go left for a few yards to reach Lochan nan Nathrach ④.

After leaving the lochan, follow the track round to the left as it winds gently uphill. Where a clear cross-track comes in from the right, watch carefully for an opening on the left leading to a small path on the line of a former railway used for extracting timber. There are fine views of Loch Morlich on this stretch. After crossing a burn by a neat wooden footbridge, go left for a short distance to meet the track used at the start of the walk. Cross the track, walk down to the loch and turn right on the small path at its edge.

Past the corner of the loch, follow the path left to pick up the white waymarks of another trail. Turn left over a footbridge to reach the Abhainn Ruigh-eunachan (river with bird-rich delta), with a sandy beach opposite. Follow the path right beside the burn and through the forest until you reach a post numbered 5. Turn left here to reach the forest track leading back to the car park.

POINTS OF INTEREST

① Glenmore Forest Park, run by the Forestry Commission, covers a large area on the Cairngorm foothills. Much of the forest is commercial spruce and fir planting, but there is also an important remnant of the old Caledonian pine forest, and a long-term improvement programme aims to consolidate and extend this native pine wood. Birds in the forest range from the seed-eating crossbill up to the large capercaillie. There is a forest visitor centre on the north side of Loch Morlich.

② Loch Morlich is much used for recreation, and you will see sailing, windsurfing and canoeing. Most of the activity is centred on the northern side of the loch, alongside the road: this southern shore is much quieter. If you are very lucky you may see an osprey fishing – they occasionally use this loch as well as their better-known haunt at Loch Garten, a few miles away.

③ The adjoining estate of Rothiemurchus has been in the hands of the Grant family for 500 years. It extends from near Aviemore up to the Cairngorm summits, and has a visitor centre at Inverdruie.

④ Lochan nan Nathrach – the Serpent's Loch – is a secretive little place almost hidden in the trees. It may take its name from its shape, which is a serpentine figure-of-eight. A picnic table is provided, and this is a good place to stop and listen to the sounds of the forest.

The building in fact dates only from 1918, and was built as part of the movement to provide 'a land fit for heroes' in the aftermath of the Great War. The ground here is fertile, but the lack of road access told, and the building was only occupied for a dozen years before assuming its present use.

The fine artistic decoration round the doors and windows was done by the warden from 1986 to 1991, a young Canadian whose affinity with the works of J R R Tolkien is clear! The hostel has no electricity and all supplies must be walked in, but its superb location and atmosphere more than make up for any lack of facilities. Beyond Craig, the path extends to Diabaig on Loch Torridon.

▲ Ancient pine woods enclose the River Affric as it flows eastwards over the Dog Falls

WALK 9

UP TO COIRE LOCH

Fascinating scenery and a lively river form part of this walk, which is about 60 minutes' drive away from Inverness. Some parts of the walk will not suit the inexperienced, elderly or unfit. Stout shoes or boots should be worn.

ROUTE DIRECTIONS

Approx. 2¼ miles. Allow 1½ hours
Start from the Dog Fall car park on the north bank of the River Affric (grid ref. NH284283) ①.

Follow the riverside path downstream for about 330yds, then cross the road and continue on a higher level until the path returns to the river gorge and a graceful footbridge across it.

Cross the river and climb a high stile over the deer fence, then fork right on a narrow path under birch trees. These give way to pines as the path climbs very steeply to meet a forest road.

Turn left along the forest road and in approximately

½ mile left again at the path signposted for Coire Loch. In a further 250yds make a third left turn (signed Forest Walk) ②.

From the loch, continue following the path as it descends steeply to the river bank again. Return to the car park by the roadside, stopping to enjoy views of the gorge from the various viewpoints.

POINTS OF INTEREST

① Glen Affric, one of Scotland's loveliest glens, extends into the lonely mountain country on the former borders of Ross and Cromarty. It is noted for its richly wooded scenery – old pine woods, long pre-dating the extensive areas of imported conifers that now cover much of the Highlands.

② Coire Loch is a tiny loch set in a secret bowl-shaped hollow, trapped between high ridges and gnarled sentinel pines. These display massive stabbed bark (the fissures are home for a hundred different insects) and delicate lichen structures. They are the direct descendants of the first plants to colonise this area when the last pocket of ice left its sheltering hollow some 10,000 years ago. It is not necessary to be a biologist or an earth scientist to appreciate the beautiful silence of the still waters of the loch. A bench high above it offers the chance to enjoy the surroundings.

WALK 10

THE BRAES OF MAR

A high viewpoint with lovely views is followed by an historic Deeside castle.

ROUTE DIRECTIONS

Approx. 3 miles. Allow 2 hours
The walk starts from the car park in Braemar (grid ref. NO152913).

Note: the upper part of the path on Creag Choinnich is steep, rocky and rough in places, and boots are recommended.

Before leaving the car park, take time to look at the ruins of Kindrochit Castle ①.

Leave the car park by the right-hand set of steps, past Invercauld Galleries. Cross the Glenshee road to see the house where Robert Louis Stevenson wrote the first draft of *Treasure Island* and then turn left.

Take the first turning right, past St Margaret's Church, and continue along this road passing the offices of the Braemar Royal Highland Society, which organises the famous gathering held on the first Saturday of September each year and usually attended by the Queen and other members of the Royal Family.

Where the road bends right, leave it on the left to cross a stile into woodland. Go straight ahead following the signpost for Creag Choinnich. Continue through this pleasant open pine wood, and at a crosspath again go ahead and begin climbing in earnest.

The path leaves the wood for the last steep climb to the summit. The views are opening up all the time so there is plenty of excuse for a pause! On reaching the large cairn at the summit of Creag Choinnich ② you will agree that the effort is well rewarded by the splendid panorama.

Return by the same path as far as the crosspath (red and yellow waymark) and turn right. This is the Queen's Drive, one of Queen Victoria's favourite pony walks. Follow this attractive path through the wood, crossing two clearings with curious dwarf trees. Leave the wood by a stile and continue between fences to reach a viewpoint indicator giving information on the landscape and wildlife of the area. The path drops down to the A93 road. Turn left and in 150yds reach the entrance to Braemar Castle ③.

After leaving the castle, continue along the road passing the graveyard and the old toll house, built to collect tolls on the turnpike road which was completed in 1863. Cross the road at the Invercauld Arms Hotel to see the stone marking the raising of the standard during the 1715 Rising ④.

Continue past the Festival Theatre to return to the car park.

POINTS OF INTEREST

① It is believed that the original Kindrochit Castle was erected by King Malcolm Canmore (1057–93), and later extended by Robert II (1371–90). He granted it to Sir Malcolm Drummond, who was killed by bandits in 1402. The castle was later occupied by Alexander Stewart, who tried to claim the lands of Mar, but was in ruins by the mid-16th century. Kindrochit means 'bridgehead'.

② Creag Choinnich (Kenneth's Crag) may have been the site of Scotland's first hill-race. Legend has it that Malcolm Canmore held a race to the top and back from Kindrochit to establish which of his warriors was fleetest of foot. Today's visitor need not be in such a hurry, and can enjoy the superb views all around. To the east is Lochnagar, and below in the glen is Invercauld House, seat of the Farquharson family. Westward, Braemar is spread out below and the eye is drawn irresistibly up the Dee valley to the high tops of the Cairngorms beyond.

③ Braemar Castle was begun in 1628 by the Earl of Mar on the site of older fortification. It was attacked and burnt in 1689 by the 'Black Colonel', John Farquharson, and later repaired by the Government for use as a garrison after the Jacobite Risings. It returned to the Farquharsons in the early 19th century. The castle is open every day from May to early October.

④ In 1715 the Earl of Mar was one of the leaders of the Rising attempting to restore the Stuarts to the throne of Great Britain. The standard calling the clans to arms was raised here, but the rebellion fizzled out in the inconclusive Battle of Sheriffmuir (near Stirling), not least because of the vacillations of Mar, who earned the nickname 'Bobbing John'.

▼ Braemar village in the Dee valley

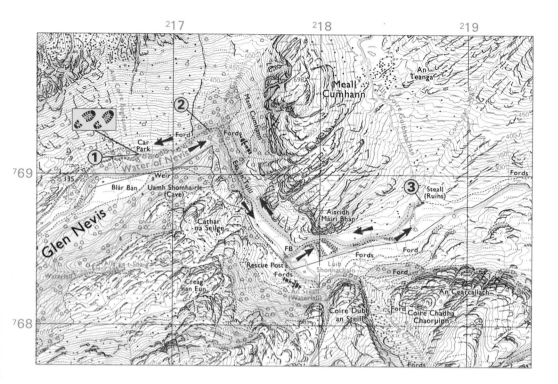

BELOW BEN NEVIS

This classic walk is on clear but stony footpaths which pass through a gorge of Himalayan proportions to visit one of the country's best waterfalls. Stout footwear is advisable and the drops along the path demand caution.

ROUTE DIRECTIONS

Approx. 3 miles. Allow 2 hours
Start from the car park at the head of Glen Nevis (grid ref. NN168691).

Beside the car park is the famous 'waterslide' which descends 1,500ft off Ben Nevis, the highest mountain in Britain ①.

From the car park follow the footpath along into the gorge ②.

The more adventurous can cross a three-wire suspension bridge to pass Steall Cottage (a locked climbing hut) and reach the foot of the falls; everyone can wander along the right of way for ¼ mile ③.

The path eastwards does not meet a metalled road again before two or three *days* of walking, so it is best to return from Steall!

At the mouth of the gorge, going back, there is a more challenging alternative path for experienced walkers. Turn up the slope by the barely visible zigzags and follow it along and down again. From the highest point the fine view is at its most extensive. This path merges with the outward one to lead back to the car park.

POINTS OF INTEREST

① The road up Glen Nevis from Fort William (where there is an interesting museum) is twisty and narrow with some fine scenery. The road crosses the river at Polldubh and it is worth stopping to see some more falls here. Polldubh Crags above the road here are popular with rock-climbers.

② There is a slightly awkward stream to cross, and later the remains of a 23-year-old rockfall lie on the path. Where the gorge narrows, note the carved whorls and curves of water action on the rocks, even 100ft overhead. When the water is in spate this can be an awesome place. In drier conditions you will notice that the rocks

in the river bed have been carved into fantastic shapes by the river.

There is a sudden change of atmosphere as you leave the gorge to stroll across a green and placid meadow, beyond which are seen the great Steall Falls, which tumble down from the Mamore Range in a sweeping veil. A wet day ensures the most spectacular scene, so do not be put off if it is raining.

③ Although it can be rather muddy here at times, the Steall ruins, beside a river of many small falls, are a point of interest at this charming spot.

WALK 12

LOCH FASKALLY

This walk explores the area around Loch Faskally, near the attractive town of Pitlochry, and includes the famous Pass of Killiecrankie, site of a fierce battle in 1689.

ROUTE DIRECTIONS

Approx. 6 miles (9 miles with extension). Allow 4 hours
Start from the car park at the dam in Pitlochry (grid ref. NN935577).

The dam, with its fishladder that allows salmon to pass upriver, can be visited. Take the path signposted to Faskally and Killiecrankie and walk along beside Loch Faskally ①.

Leave the lochside and walk up beside a fence and then a stone dyke to reach a minor road. Turn left past the Green Park Hotel and resume the lochside path. Follow the path uphill and then underneath the bridge carrying the A9 over the loch ②.

At a path junction, follow the signs marked Killiecrankie to the right and climb steeply for a short while before enjoying the walk through Faskally Woods. The woodland is varied, with some splendid old trees mixing with more recent plantations of spruce, pine and birch.

The path eventually winds downhill and passes Loch Dunmore (on your right). At a junction here, turn left and join the road leading to the Freshwater Fisheries Laboratory. Just before the laboratory, take the signposted path on the left beside the water again, with Faskally House on the right ③.

Continue, now beside the River Garry, pass under the rather stark modern bridge taking the B8019 road to Loch Rannoch, and in a further ¼ mile reach a footbridge over the Garry ④.

An optional extension can be walked from here to take in the Killiecrankie Visitor Centre. Otherwise, cross over the bridge, turn left on a surfaced path (part of an old road) and then turn left along the signposted riverside path. After about ½ mile, climb some steps and walk through woods to join the Tummel, the other river feeding Loch Faskally. On the small pier below is a cairn marking a visit here by Queen Victoria in 1844. Continue beside the Tummel on the marked nature trail ⑤, following the signs to Coronation Bridge.

Once over the Coronation Bridge, follow the road back to the Clunie footbridge over Loch Faskally ⑥.

Cross the loch by the footbridge and resume your outward route to return to the dam and car park.

POINTS OF INTEREST

① This whole area is noted for its beautiful trees. They are especially fine in the autumn months, when the colours are magnificent. Loch Faskally was man-made as part of a large hydroelectric power scheme, but is none the less attractive for that.

② The bridge won a Saltire Society award for its design and construction in 1981. The Clunie footbridge next to it – and rather overshadowed by its big new brother – dates from 1950 and replaced an older bridge which took the road over the River Tummel here before the loch was created.

③ Faskally House is used by Strathclyde Regional Council as an outdoor centre. The walk from here takes you along beside the rushing River Garry and into the Pass of Killiecrankie. Rising above and to the right is Ben Vrackie – just under 3,000ft and a popular walk from Pitlochry. Ben Vrackie translates as 'speckled hill' and Killiecrankie means 'wood of aspen trees'.

④ At this point you have a choice. Carrying on for another mile or so would lead you to the National Trust for Scotland visitor centre at Killiecrankie, which has excellent displays on the natural history of the area and also on the Battle of Killiecrankie in 1689, one of the first significant Jacobite victories. Or you can cross the Garry Bridge now and start on the return walk.

⑤ This area is known as the Linn of Tummel, meaning 'pools of the plunging stream', which could hardly be more appropriate as the river rushes over a series of lovely small waterfalls. It too is owned by the National Trust for Scotland. The falls were formerly rather higher but the river level fell when the hydropower scheme was completed.

⑥ There are fine views all along this section, and you pass the Clunie Power Station with its imposing archway entrance. It bears the names of five workmen killed during the construction of the Clunie Tunnel in 1948–49.

▼ Man-made, but not inharmonious, Loch Faskally

115

WALK 13

BEINN LORA

Beinn Lora is only 1,000ft high but from its summit there is a magnificent panorama of mountains, sea and islands. A good path leads all the way to the top.

ROUTE DIRECTIONS

Approx. 4 miles. Allow 2½ hours
Start from the Forestry Commission car park in Benderloch, just off the A828 (grid ref. NM905380).

From the car park go through the gate. At the path junction go right to start the climb. The path bends left, still climbing, and passes through a grove of superb old beech trees. At a junction, go right to reach the first viewpoint ①.

The path continues climbing steeply, crossing a small burn twice. At a junction go straight ahead (signed Beinn Lora) ②.

The path skirts an area of boggy pools where dragonflies can be seen in summer and reaches the forest edge. Go through the gate and descend half-left for a short distance to pick up the path to the summit of Beinn Lora, which can clearly be seen to the left.

Continue on this path as it winds up to the summit. Some parts may be muddy after wet weather. At the summit triangulation pillar, take in the superb views in every direction ③.

Before returning by the same route, a short walk south to the edge of the hill brings into view the dead-flat land of the Moss of Achnacree. Several prehistoric chambered cairns have been discovered here.

POINTS OF INTEREST

① From the first viewpoint the panorama is already opening up. Below is Ardmucknish Bay and the island of Lismore, whose name means 'Great Garden'. It makes an excellent day out from Oban.

② The trees here are mainly fast-growing conifers of the type extensively planted in Scotland over the past 45 years. An initial thinning takes place after about 25 years and the main crop can be taken out in 35–40 years. Being on the west coast, high winds are common, and there was considerable storm damage in this forest in the winter of 1988–89.

③ The summit panorama is quite magnificent. To the west, Mull dominates, with ships often visible in the Sound of Mull. In clear conditions, Duart Castle can be seen. The lovely island of Kerrera in Oban Bay also stands out clearly. Inland, the eye is caught by the superb upthrust of Ben Cruachan (3,695ft), and by the long curve of Loch Etive below the peak.

But it is to the west that the observer is drawn, to the ever-changing pattern of light and shade between land, sky and sea. To be here as the sun is setting, glowing like fire on the sea, is to understand the ancient belief that out there, beyond the sunset, was Tir nan Og – the land of eternal youth.

WALK 14

AROUND LOCH KATRINE

This walk around the west end of Loch Katrine passes the house where Rob Roy MacGregor

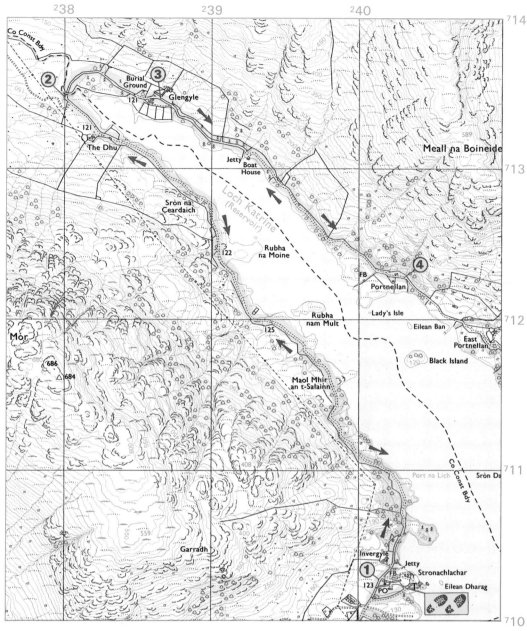

was born. The walk is on a metalled road all the way, so normal footwear can be worn.

ROUTE DIRECTIONS

Approx. 10 miles. Allow 4 hours
Start from the pier at Stronachlachar (grid ref. NN404102).

From the pier, go back up the road for about 400yds and turn right at the junction (signed 'No Unauthorised Vehicles'). Walk through the houses to reach the lochside road ①.

Continue along the road – which carries very little traffic – to the head of the loch ②.

Cross the bridge and continue to Glengyle House and the Clan Gregor burial ground ③.

Continue for another mile or so to Portnellan ④.

Return to Stronachlachar by the same route.

POINTS OF INTEREST

① The houses at Stronachlachar (headland of the mason) were built when Loch Katrine was greatly enlarged as part of a major scheme to supply water to Glasgow. Just offshore is Eilean Dharag, also known as the Factor's Island from the time when the Duke of Montrose's factor, Graham of Killearn, was held to ransom here by Rob Roy.

② From the head of the loch you can look up Glen Gyle; a few rough miles to the west is the north end of Loch Lomond and the drovers' inn at Inverarnan. Above the glen to the north is the Bealach nan Corp (pass of the bodies), indicating that a funeral route came this way. The large and rather obtrusive pylons carry power from the Ben Cruachan hydroelectric scheme.

③ Glengyle was the birthplace of Rob Roy (Red Robert) MacGregor in.1671. He has a rather fearsome reputation but in those harsh times it paid to be a jump ahead of the opposition, even if the means employed did not always accord with the law. For most of his life Rob was forced to take his mother's name of Campbell, the name of MacGregor being banned or 'proscribed' by the Government. Little wonder that the clan's rallying cry was 'MacGregor Despite Them'. Rob operated as a cattle-dealer, and the term 'blackmail' originates from those times, referring to the 'mail' or payment taken for safeguarding the passage of the black cattle.

Just before you reach the house, divert left uphill a short way to see the Clan Gregor burial ground. Rob Roy's nephew, Gregor of the Black Knee, is among the MacGregors buried here.

④ Just past Portnellan is another graveyard, the stones having been moved at the time the loch was enlarged. William Wordsworth wrote a poem, *Rob Roy's Grave*, after visiting this site, but he was misinformed, for Rob is buried in Balquhidder churchyard.

Page numbers in bold type indicate main entries.

ACKNOWLEDGEMENTS

The Automobile Association wishes to thank the following
photographers, libraries and associations for their
assistance in the preparation of this book.

Highland & Islands Development Board 24 Cowal Gathering, 27 Gairloch Fishing Fleet, 28 Oil Rig;
International Photobank Cover Eilean Donan Castle; *Nature Photographer Ltd* 15 Chequered Skipper
(D Smith), 16 Golden Eagle (F V Blackburn), 16 Woods, 17 Pearl Bordered Fritillary (M R Hall), 19 Salmon
(C Palmer), 19 Rose Bay Willow Herb (E A Janes), 20 Fulmar (M Colbeck); *Scottish Tourist Board* 25
Tartan; *The Mansell Collection* 6 Book of Kells, 8 Battle of Culloden, 27 Aberdeen

All remaining pictures are held in the Associations own library (AA PHOTO LIBRARY) with contributions
from: M Adelman, J Beazley, J Carnie, D Corrance, A Grierly, D Hardley, B Johnson, R Weir

Other Ordnance Survey Maps of the Scottish Highlands

How to get there with Routemaster and Routeplanner Maps

Reach the Scottish Highlands from Glasgow, Edinburgh, Inverness and Aberdeen using Ordnance
Survey Routemaster Map sheets 2 and 4. Alternatively plan your route using the Ordnance Survey
Routeplanner Map which covers the whole country on one map sheet.

Exploring with Landranger, Tourist and Outdoor Leisure Maps

Landranger series
1¼ inches to one mile or 1:50,000 scale
These maps cover the whole of Britain and are
good for local motoring and walking. Each
contains tourist information such as parking,
picnic places and viewpoints, camping and caravan
sites.
Sheets 7 to 69 cover the area.

Outdoor Leisure Maps
2½ inches to one mile or 1:25,000 scale
These maps for walkers show the popular leisure
and recreation areas of Britain. They are packed
with detail and include tourist information such
as camping and caravan sites, youth hostels,

picnic areas and footpaths. There are two Outdoor
Leisure Maps for the Scottish Highlands area.
Sheet 8 – The Cuillin & Torridon Hills
Sheet 3 – Aviemore & the Cairngorms (showing
Ben Macdui, Braeriach, Cairn Toul and Cairn
Gorm)

Touring Map and Guide of Scotland
This map covers all of Scotland at a scale of 1
inch to 8 miles. The map contains Tourist
Information such as camping and caravan sites,
country parks and golf courses. On the reverse of
the map is a comprehensive illustrated guide
giving lots of ideas on where to go and what to
see.

Other titles available in this series are:
Brecon Beacons; Channel Islands; Cornwall; Cotswolds; Days out from London; Devon and Exmoor;
East Anglia; Forest of Dean and Wye Valley; Ireland; Isle of Wight; Lake District; New Forest;
Northumbria; North York Moors; Peak District; Snowdonia; South Downs; Wessex; Yorkshire Dales.